Video Poker

Bob Dancer
Liam W. Daily

Winner's Guides

Volume 2

A Winner's Guide to Double Bonus

Bob Dancer and Liam W. Daily

Video Poker Winner's Guides

**Bob Dancer
Liam W. Daily**

Volume 1 – Jacks or Better

(including 9/6, 8/6, 9/5, 8/5 with quads = 35, and 8/5 Bonus)

Volume 2 – Double Bonus

(including 10/7, 9/7, and 10/7 with straight flush = 80)

(Upcoming Titles in 2003)

Volume 3 – Full Pay Deuces Wild

**(also including "*pseudo* Full Pay Deuces Wild" with wild royal = 20
and 5-of-a-kind = 12)**

Volume 4 – NSU Deuces Wild

(including 16/10/4/4/3 "Not So Ugly" and 15/9/4/4/3 "Ugly Ducks")

Volume 5 – Pick'em Poker

Copyright © 2003, Compton Dancer Consulting Inc.
3690 S. Eastern Avenue, Suite 213
Las Vegas, NV 89109
702-214-9500

ISBN 0-9727592-1-2

TABLE OF CONTENTS

Chapter 1.   **Introduction**   5

   1.1.   The Features of Double Bonus   6

   1.2.   How can casinos afford to offer 100%+ games?   9

   1.3.   Why is Double Bonus so difficult?   10

   1.4.   A volatile day in the life of a Double Bonus player.   11

   1.5.   Remember the Basics   12

   1.6.   Strategy

       1.6.1.   How preferred strategy is determined   16
       1.6.2.   "Top down" strategy   17
       1.6.3.   The four levels of strategy   18
       1.6.4.   General Principles   19

Chapter 2.   **Level 1: "Beginner Strategy"**

   2.1.   Beginner Strategy Table   20

   2.2.   Seven General Principles of Double Bonus Strategy   21

   2.3.   Beginner Strategy Examples   28

   2.4.   Beginner Strategy Practice Session   32

Chapter 3.   **Level 2: "Recreational Strategy"**

   3.1.   Recreational Strategy Table   33

   3.2.   Continuation of General Principles   34

   3.3.   Recreational Strategy Examples   41

   3.4.   Recreational Strategy Practice Session   46

Chapter 4.   **Level 3: Introduction to "Basic Strategy"**

   4.1.   The Meaning of "Basic Strategy"   47

   4.2.   Notation

       4.2.1.   Hand type notation   48
       4.2.2.   Suited versus unsuited cards   49
       4.2.3.   Insides   49
       4.2.4.   The problem with SF3s   51
       4.2.5.   The meaning of ">" and "<"   52

Chapter 5. Level 3: "Basic Strategy" for 10/7 and 9/7

   5.1.   Basic Strategy Table   53

   5.2.   The Relationships between High Pairs, RF3, and FL4   54

       5.2.1. Relationship when only two are present.   56
       5.2.2. Relationship when all three are present.   57

   5.3   Summary of the General Principles   60

   5.4.   Exceptions, Extensions, and Additions to the General Principles   62

   5.5.   Basic Strategy Examples   64

   5.6.   Basic Strategy Practice Session

       5.6.1. Basic Strategy Practice Session part 1   68
       5.6.1. Basic Strategy Practice Session part 2   69

Chapter 6. Level 4: "Advanced Strategy" for 10/7 and 9/7

   6.1.   Additional Instructions and Notation for Level 4

       6.1.1. Main and secondary references   70
       6.1.2. Penalty cards   70
       6.1.3. "When" versus "With"   72
       6.1.4. Square brackets and curved brackets   73

   6.2.   Advanced Strategy Table   74

   6.3.   Exceptions to Basic Strategy   75

   6.4.   Advanced Strategy Examples   82

   6.5.   Advanced Strategy Practice Session   87

Chapter 7. Level 3: "Basic Strategy" for 10/7/80

   7.1.   Introduction to 10/7/80   88

   7.2.   Basic Strategy Table for 10/7/80   90

   7.3.   Similarities Between SF-50 and SF-80 Basic Strategies   91

   7.4.   Differences Between SF-50 and SF-80 Basic Strategies   93

   7.5.   Basic Strategy Examples for 10/7/80   96

   7.6.   Basic Strategy Practice Session for 10/7/80   99

Chapter 8. Level 4: "Advanced Strategy" for 10/7/80

   8.1.   Advanced Strategy Table for 10/7/80   100

   8.2.   Exceptions to the Basic Strategy for 10/7/80   101

   8.3.   Differences between SF-50 and SF-80 Advanced Strategies   106

   8.4.   Advanced Strategy Examples for 10/7/80   107

   8.5.   Advanced Strategy Practice Session for 10/7/80   110

Appendix. SF2 versus Five New Cards in 10/7/80   111

Chapter 1

Introduction

Welcome to Volume 2 of the Dancer/Daily Video Poker Winner's Guides. This volume covers the game of Double Bonus. Although it is not necessary that you should have read Volume 1 on Jacks or Better, you will find this volume a lot easier if you have at least mastered the basics of Jacks or Better. Of all the games covered in this series, Double Bonus is the most difficult to master at a high strategy level. However, although difficult, this Guide gives you the tools to be able to play the game "perfectly" without recourse to impossible-to-remember appendices.

Considerable skill is required to play Double Bonus well. There are some players, including the authors, who actually enjoy the complexities of the game. Compared to Jacks or Better, a much greater proportion of hands require you to pause and think. To play Double Bonus well, you must be "on your toes" the whole time.

Some players "tolerate" the complexities of Double Bonus in order to achieve the high return that is available. At the time of writing in late 2002, the game of Double Bonus that pays 10 for a full house and 7 for a flush (known simply as 10/7) has been the single most important game for dollar players in Las Vegas. Players who wish to play for this stake and have no desire to play a game where the casino has the edge MUST learn this game. Although Full Pay Deuces Wild is an easier game that returns over ½% more, and is also considered by many to be more fun, it looks as though it will NEVER be available for dollars anymore. Quarter players who have a choice between 10/7 Double Bonus and full pay Deuces Wild usually choose the latter – but it's expected that the Double Bonus game will be around a lot longer at many casinos so wise quarter players are learning both games.

Many players are attracted to the very high payouts on 4-of-a-kinds, known as quads. With the maximum 5-coin bet, quad aces pay 800; quad 2s – 4s pay 400, while all other quads pay 250. This compares with 125 on all quads in most games of Jacks or Better. Even if you are down by, say, four or five hundred coins, your situation can quickly be turned around by quad aces or a couple of sets of quad 2s – 4s. Unfortunately, when the higher paying quads fail to appear as often as expected, you must expect very expensive losing streaks. In Bob Dancer's now-out-of-print "10/7 Double Bonus Video Poker Report," he stated at the beginning, "This is an ugly game."

Many players who are attracted by the high payouts on quads crave the excitement that this brings. In general, such people will not be turned on by the difficult task of mastering this Winner's Guide. The question we pose to you at the beginning is, "Is this good news or bad?" We suggest it is good news. This is a game that rewards serious students very well, while those not willing to study will not do so well. The non-studiers will allow the casino to earn enough money to support the better players. The fact that you have this Winner's Guide in your hands implies that you are at least considering studying this game. We encourage you to plow ahead. The game of Double Bonus has been good to both the authors and we invite you to join us in profiting from it.

Another benefit from learning this game comes from mastering the influences of penalty cards. There will surely be dozens (possibly hundreds) of new video poker games appearing in casinos in the next several years – and these Winner's Guides will be written about very few of them. After you have studied this volume enough to understand the concepts of flush penalties, straight penalties, high-pair penalties and others, you'll be able to recognize more easily these same situations in other games. Once you have mastered a game like Double Bonus, you'll be able to master other games much more quickly and thoroughly than you could if you had never attempted to master Double Bonus in the first place. If you are planning to play video poker at least semi-regularly for a period of years, the time invested learning this game is time well spent.

1.1. The Features of Double Bonus

We are going to begin this section with a table of the payouts on various games of Double Bonus, together with a couple of extra games for the purpose of comparison. The table gives the payouts for a single coin bet, with the exception of the payout on the royal flush. Normally, a royal flush returns 4,000 with a 5-coin maximum bet. This divides out to 800 per coin. However, if you actually bet less than five coins, the return per coin bet is generally only 250. Throughout these Guides, we use the following notation: A = ace; K = king; Q = queen; J = jack; and T = 10.

	A	B	C	D	E	F	G
	10/7 Double Bonus	9/7 Double Bonus	10/7/80 Double Bonus	9/6/5 Double Bonus	9/6/4 Double Bonus	8/5 Bonus Poker	9/6 Jacks or Better
Royal Flush	800	800	800	800	800	800	800
Straight Flush	50	50	80	50	50	50	50
4-of-a-kind As	160	160	160	160	160	80	25
4-of-a-kind 2s – 4s	80	80	80	80	80	40	25
4-of-a-kind 5s – Ks	50	50	50	50	50	25	25
Full House	10	9	10	9	9	8	9
Flush	7	7	7	6	6	5	6
Straight	5	5	5	5	4	4	4
3-of-a-kind	3	3	3	3	3	3	3
Two Pair	1	1	1	1	1	2	2
Jacks or Better	1	1	1	1	1	1	1
Theoretical Return	100.17%	99.11%	100.52%	97.81%	96.38%	99.17%	99.54%

The bottom line in the above table gives the theoretical returns.[1] These returns are statistical expectations. In layman's terms, these returns assume that the player receives an average share of all payouts, including infrequent jackpots such as royal flushes and quads. In practical terms, this is a long-term concept in which a very large number of hands are played. These expected returns also assume "computer perfect" play, which is presented in this Guide in Level 4: "Advanced Strategy."

Examples of the various Double Bonus games are given in columns A – E. There are two main features that distinguish games of Double Bonus. The first is the payouts on quads. They pay 160 per unit bet for quad aces, 80 for quad 2s – 4s, and 50 for all other quads. With the maximum 5-coin bet, these translate into 800, 400, and 250 respectively. The second feature is that, as well as paying even money for pairs of jacks or better, they also only pay even money for two pair.

Despite paying even money on pairs of jacks or better, we do not consider Double Bonus to be a game of "Jacks or Better" as covered in Volume 1 of these Guides. We restrict the use of "Jacks or Better" to games that, as well as paying even money on pairs of jacks or better, pay 2 for 1 on two pair, and also have the same payout on all quads. (We covered Bonus Poker in Volume 1 simply because its strategy is very close indeed to the traditional game of 8/5 Jacks or Better.) We mention this in order to avoid any confusion when we compare Double Bonus to Jacks or Better in this Guide.

The first three columns in the table (A, B, and C) are the games covered in this Guide. The games in columns D and E are not covered even though they represent the most common versions of Double Bonus found around the country. There are two reasons for not covering them. First, their strategies are very different from any game where flushes return 7 for 1, and, second, their returns are sufficiently negative such that no "winning" player would consider them.

The game in column F is Bonus Poker, which was covered in Volume 1. We include this pay schedule because it is this game from which the name "Double Bonus" was derived. In Bonus Poker, quad aces pay 80, quad 2s – 4s pay 40, while all other quads pay the "normal" 25. Double Bonus games pay exactly double these amounts for quads. Bonus Poker is also worthy of discussion because players who like the excitement of the bonus payout on quads may be attracted to both games.

We have also included in column G the pay schedule for the traditional game of 9/6 Jacks or Better. The reason for this is to show the potential pitfalls in casually perusing pay schedules in an attempt to assess which game "looks" more attractive. The pay schedule for 9/6 Jacks or Better has identical payouts on a full house, flush, and straight (as well as the returns for jacks or better, 3-of-a-kind, straight flush, and royal flush) as the 9/6 version of Double Bonus given in column E. Some people have

---

[1] All numerical amounts cited in this Guide were verified using **Bob Dancer Presents WinPoker**. This is an award-winning computer trainer created by Dean Zamzow. **WinPoker** is by far the best tool to use to practice Double Bonus or any other video poker game. Copies may be ordered at www.zamzone.com, www.bobdancer.com, or from wherever you purchased this report.

the view that it is good to find a game that pays "9/6." While this is true of Jacks or Better, it is not true of Double Bonus.

If players casually compare the pay schedules in columns E and G, 9/6 Double Bonus may strike them as more favorable than 9/6 Jacks or Better. After all, the payouts on quads are so much more attractive, and all you give up to get them is a reduction of one in the payout on two pair. This is a huge mistake. As you will see from the theoretical returns, this 9/6 game of Double Bonus only returns 96.38%, which gives you no chance of being a winner in the long term. In contrast, 9/6 Jacks or Better returns 99.54%, which gives the possibility of the player having the advantage when combined with decent slot-club cash back and other promotional or complimentary factors.

The reason why Double Bonus is able to offer such attractive returns on quads is precisely because it only pays even money on two pair. Approximately 12.5% of all hands turn into two pair. When their payout is reduced from 2 to 1, the total return on the game is therefore reduced by 12.5%. Although the premiums on quads make up some of the difference, you are still left with a return on 9/6/4 Double Bonus of 96.38%, which is more than 3% less than on 9/6 Jacks or Better.

Moving from column E to column D, we have 9/6 Double Bonus with the payout on the straight increased from 4 to 5. When strategy is adjusted to reflect this increase, the frequency of straights rises from around 1.3% to 1.5%. This increases the theoretical return on the game from 96.38% to 97.81%, which is still unacceptably low for players desiring to win.

Similarly, when the payout on the flush is increased from 6 to 7 and strategy is adjusted to reflect this, the frequency of flushes increases from 1.1% to 1.5%. Again, the total return of the game is increased by a figure that is in between these two amounts. In column B, the game of 9/7 Double Bonus is shown to have a return of 99.11%. You will notice that we refer to this game as simply "9/7" rather than "9/7/5". All the games covered in this Winner's Guide pay 5 on the straight. This figure is critical to the strategy and critical to the return.

It is interesting to note the similarity in the returns on 9/7 Double Bonus and 8/5 Bonus Poker. However, although 9/7 Double Bonus and 8/5 Bonus Poker have very similar returns, they have very different strategies. Also, you can expect much wider swings in Double Bonus than in Bonus Poker.

Full houses result from around 1.1% of all hands dealt and the exact value of the full house has little effect on strategy. The return on 10/7 Double Bonus is given in column A. It is approximately 1.1% greater than on 9/7 at 100.17%. This means that, in the long term assuming perfect play, the player has an advantage over the casino, even before other benefits such as cash back, special promotions, complimentaries, etc. are considered.

The game presented in column C is a game that can sometimes be found on Bally GameMaker machines. With a 5-coin bet, the payout on a straight flush is raised from 250 to 400 and the theoretical return is raised to 100.52%. We call this game 10/7/80, where the 80 equals the payout on the straight flush per unit bet. However, the payout on the straight flush on this game if you actually play less than five coins is 50. Be sure to look at the 5-coin payout schedule as the single-coin schedule will lead you to think that you are playing on a lesser game.

1.2. How can casinos afford to offer 100%+ games?

In Volume I of the Winner's Guides, we asked the question, "How can you be a winner when the games return less than 100%?" This question is turned on its head in Double Bonus. How can casinos offer games that return more than 100%? As we write this in late 2002, there are several hundred machines offering 10/7 Double Bonus with a return of 100.17% that are to be found in casinos in the greater Las Vegas area. Most of these games are for quarters, but they can also be found in half dollar, dollar, and two dollar denominations. Many of these casinos offer same-day slot-club cash back and most of the others offer a "checks in the mail" form of cash rebate.

The answer to this question is that Double Bonus is a very difficult game indeed. Most players do not take the time to learn to play it well. For this reason, casinos find the game profitable to them. This is a stable relationship. The casinos can truthfully advertise "over 100%" games and yet still make money on them because of player ineptitude. For the serious player, this is wonderful news. The game is likely to survive in casinos and time spent learning the game will pay dividends for a long time to come. 10/7 Double Bonus has been the game-of-choice for winning players in Las Vegas who like to play $1 or $2 denomination.

Many video poker players with a little knowledge know that Double Bonus can be a profitable game. This anecdotal appraisal is akin to the idea that it is good to find a game paying 9/6 on the full house and the flush. Both notions are true only in special situations. If the game of Double Bonus pays 10/7 and you know the strategy, the first notion is correct. If you have a Jacks or Better game that pays 9/6 and also 2 for 1 on two pair, the second notion is correct. However, put these two notions together and you have a windfall for the casinos where the player with only a little knowledge may find a 9/6 game of Double Bonus and think that it is worth playing.

Many players use some sort of a generic strategy that they play on all games of video poker. In fact, you may see players frequently switching between games without any apparent thought to how strategy should change. Perhaps the player thinks that you should "never draw to an inside straight." Perhaps the player thinks that, when quad aces pay so much, you should always keep a pair of aces rather than two pair. Combine some anecdotal information with some intuition and you get a situation in which the casino makes a good profit on games where the theoretical return is in favor of the player. However well these Winner's Guides sell, there will always be an overwhelming proportion of players who play Double Bonus badly.

1.3. Why is Double Bonus so difficult?

When we say that Double Bonus is a difficult game to play, we mean that it is difficult to achieve the full potential of the game. It is not difficult to play and achieve close to break-even. A surprising fact that was first noted by Bob Dancer is that, if you play 10/7 Double Bonus using 9/6 Jacks or Better strategy, the expected return is 99.63%, which is higher that the 99.54% return on Jacks or Better. This does not mean that you should immediately switch from 9/6 Jacks or Better to 10/7 Double Bonus if the game is available. Whatever strategy you use, Double Bonus is a great deal more volatile than Jacks or Better. If you have a limited stake that you wish to last as long as possible and only know the strategy for Jacks or Better, you are probably better off sticking to 9/6 Jacks or Better. If on the other hand you are an "action junkie" who craves excitement, Double Bonus will take you on a much wilder ride.

It is possible to raise this 99.63% return quite a bit closer to break even with just the few simple changes in strategy that are given in Level 1: "Beginner Strategy." However, if you want to play at an advantage over the casino, you will need to consider hand options that are not even considered in Jacks or Better. Owing primarily to the higher payouts on the flush and straight, there are many more hand options that need to be considered in Double Bonus than in Jacks or Better. These include 3-card flushes, non-consecutive 4-card straights with less than three high cards, and the 3-card straight, QJT.

In Jacks or Better, there is a straightforward relationship in the top portion of the strategy tables between the higher-ranking hand types. This relationship remains pretty much unchanged at all strategy levels. Included in this is the relationship that a high pair is more valuable than a 3-card royal flush, which is more valuable than a 4-card flush. In Double Bonus, high pairs are worth less than they are in Jacks or Better. The impact of the higher values of full houses and quads is more than offset by the reduction in the payout on two pair. In contrast, the return on a 4-card flush is raised significantly because of the 7 for 1 payout on the flush. The return on a 3-card royal is raised but by a smaller amount due to the higher payouts on both the flush and the straight. The result is that these three combinations are neck and neck in value. Depending on the particular situation, any one of the three may be the preferred combination. There is no single easy relationship between them as there is in Jacks or Better.

Another impact of the higher return on flushes is that it is often appropriate to hold 3-card flushes in Double Bonus, even though this is never done in Jacks or Better unless the three cards to the flush are close enough to each other to be part of the same straight flush or royal flush. Also, all 3-card and 4-card straight flushes are worth more in Double Bonus than in Jacks or Better. It is easy to remember in Jacks or Better that you only hold a 3-card straight flush with two gaps and no high cards if there is absolutely nothing else worth holding. In Double Bonus, it is raised off the floor and has a complex relationship with single high cards and even high cards with suited Ts.

In Jacks or Better, 4-card straights that have a gap are only ever held if they have a minimum of three high cards. With the straight paying 5 rather than 4 in Double Bonus, it can be appropriate to hold a non-consecutive 4-card straight no matter how many high cards are in it.

If you are dealt the hand 3♣ 4♦ 5♥ 9♣ A♣, it is an easy decision in Jacks or Better to hold the A♣. However, in Double Bonus, you also need to consider the 3-card flush, 3♣ 9♣ A♣, and the non-consecutive 4-card straight, 3♣ 4♦ 5♥ A♣. There are many hands like this where Jacks or Better strategy would lead you to hold the second best or even third best option.

1.4. A volatile day in the life of a Double Bonus player.

You don't need to have much experience with video poker to know that royal flushes are rare events. However, when you are playing Double Bonus, there is a reasonable chance that you may connect on quad aces during a day's play. Even if you are already several hundred coins down, you may think that it is okay because the 800-coin win on quad aces hasn't had time to arrive yet, but, when it does, you will be back up again.

In a full day of 8 to 10 hours' play, you can expect to play around 5,000 hands. By coincidence, this is the average frequency of quad aces (and, for that matter, quad deuces in Deuces Wild). This does not mean that you are bound to hit aces in a full day's play. There is a 37% chance that you will not get quad aces in 5,000 hands, which is offset by the possibility that you will get more than one set. You can also expect to get between two and three sets of the premium quads, 2s – 4s, during that same session of 5,000 hands.

We mentioned before that, in a sense, the bonuses on quads are paid for out of the even money rather than 2 for 1 payout on two pair. The impact on volatility of the even money on two pair is of huge importance. In the course of 5,000 hands, the expectation is to get 627 sets of two pairs. Of course, you are unlikely to get this exact number, but you can be fairly certain of being within around 45 of this 627 number. There is a 95% chance that you will be between 2,900 and 3,360 coins below what you would have been if two pair had paid 2 for 1 as they do in Jacks or Better or Bonus Poker.

During a 5,000-hand playing session, you can expect to get around 75 straights, 75 flushes, and 56 full houses. With the payouts on each of these being one coin higher in 10/7 Double Bonus than in 9/6 Jacks or Better, approximately 1/3 of the shortfall from the lower payout on two pair can be expected to be made up. The remaining 2/3 needs to be made up by the higher pay for quads.

In both Jacks or Better and Bonus Poker, you can expect to make a profit (meaning two pair or better) on 24% of hands. In Double Bonus, the even money payout on two pair reduces this to 11.6% because you now need 3-or-a-kind or better. You have over a 30% chance that you will not hit better than break even in 10 hands in Double Bonus, compared to only a 9% chance in Jacks or Better.

You must expect wide swings in Double Bonus. To give you some idea of what can happen in a day's play, we ran some computer simulations. In one of these, the computer played 500 million hands of $1 denomination 10/7 Double Bonus using perfect strategy, divided up into 100,000 sessions of 5,000 hands. In 10% of these sessions, the end result was a loss of $1,995 or greater. The lowest point rather than the end point in 10% of these sessions was a loss of at least $2,330. In 5% of sessions, the figures were a minimum session loss of $2,425 and a minimum low point of $2,700. In 1% of sessions, the end loss was a minimum of $3,175 with a low point of $3,365. In other words, in an unlucky day's play, it is possible to lose three quarters of the value of a royal flush. In an unlucky week's play (assuming 25,000 hands), the simulations showed that you can lose an amount equal to two royals. If you are playing Triple Play (which is discussed later), these figures are approximately doubled.

There is really no single meaningful measure of the risk that a player is taking. Whatever volatility there is in the game in the short term tends to be overwhelmed in the long term by the percentage return on the game. A game may be very stable in the short term, but, if it has a negative return, you are doomed to lose in the long term. Alternatively, you can have a game like 10/7 Double Bonus that is very volatile in the short term, but, with the positive theoretical return (plus extras like cash back), you are very likely to be a winner in the long term – assuming, first, that you do not lose your nerve or go broke before you reach the long term, and, second, that you consistently play close-to-perfectly. We shall discuss later the importance of being able to get through these short term swings in order to reap the fruits of the positive return in the long term.

1.5. Remember the Basics

In Volume 1 of these guides, we considered in some detail many ancillary factors that are important to being a winner. To avoid too much duplication, we are only going to summarize these. The main body of these Guides looks at the complex business of playing strategy. However, being able to follow strategy tables is only one condition necessary to be a winner.

Read the pay schedule

As is true in every video poker game, learning to read the pay schedule is critical to success. The casinos that have 10/7 Double Bonus normally also have lower-paying versions. If you see a machine with a big sign over it saying "Double Bonus," it might be the 9/6/4 game that returns only 96.38%. Although you may hit four aces or a royal and win TODAY, you are doomed to give back all your winnings and more if you keep playing for long enough.

Play Maximum Coins

When you play the maximum of five coins, the payout on a royal flush is 4,000, which translates into 800 per unit bet. However, if you play less than maximum coins, the payout is normally only 250. With no change in strategy, this decreases the expected return by 1.15%. Even if you adjust strategy to take account of the lower payout, the return is still decreased by 1.06%. One of the authors' axioms for winning players is always to play maximum coins. However, we recognize that beginners may wish to play very carefully without putting much money at risk until they are accustomed to the game. If you have the choice of nickel 9/7 or quarter 10/7, it makes very little difference whether you play 5-coin nickel 9/7 or single-coin quarter 10/7. The 5-coin nickel 9/7 has a slightly higher return but is more volatile than single-coin quarter 10/7. You will be playing at a little over 99%, which isn't bad compared to most other games available in casinos. It is always better to reduce the denomination of your play before you play less than maximum coins, assuming you can find the same pay schedule in the lower denomination. We don't want to get a royal flush and feel unlucky about it.

Play within your budget

The single most important recommendation of these Guides is that the winning player must play a game and a denomination that are within his budget such that he can survive financially into the long term. In the long term, you will tend to get your share of the infrequent high-paying hands. Good strategy and good selection of games will tend to produce winners, even though there will be big swings both ways in the short term. A winner should never play a denomination that could lead to short-term losses that would influence his ability to get to the long term. In the short term, results are based primarily on luck – it is a gamble. If you risk too much money in the short term, you increase the likelihood of not making it to the long term.

As well as playing within his or her financial budget, a player must play within his emotional budget. Although the financial budgets of the authors may be of the same order, Liam W. Daily generally plays lower denominations than Bob Dancer. For Daily, losses really hurt even though he never plays at a level where losses could have any effect on his life style.

Make full use of slot clubs

Be sure to make full use of casino slot clubs. Slot clubs were invented by casinos as a marketing tool to assist them in building loyalty among their playing customers. These slot clubs typically offer such things as cash back and various comps such as rooms, meals, show tickets, airfare, etc. Several of the large casinos on the Las Vegas Strip currently offer 0.33% cash back to video poker players. There are also several off-Strip casinos that offer 0.25% cash back, with special double or triple points given periodically.

Slot clubs have real value whether they increase the return over 100% or not. Let's say that the highest returning game available to you is 9/7 Double Bonus and the slot club is giving 0.33% cash back. This gives a total return of 99.11% + 0.33% = 99.44%. If you play $30,000 through the machine (which is about ten hours of play for a dollar player), your expected loss is around $168. However, from this amount of play, casinos know from experience that the average video poker player will lose between $600 and $750. From this amount, the casino is normally willing to give back to the player between $150 and $200 in cash and comps to keep him coming back.

In general these Guides consider games that have an expected return of at least 99%. It is at this level where liberal cash back plus other promotions and comps give the player a chance of playing even with the casino, all things considered.

Double Bonus is a game that does very well in a variety of casino promotions. For a Mother's Day promotion of "double pay for four queens", would you rather receive an extra 20 or 25 coins at Deuces Wild, 125 coins at Jacks or Better, or 250 coins for Double Bonus? There have been many versions of promotions based on "earn a drawing ticket (or some other goodie) for each jackpot of $25 and higher." The versions of Double Bonus we are talking about in this Winner's Guide return 25 coins for a 5-coin straight, so dollar players earn these tickets for "straights and higher", compared to "flushes and higher" in most other dollar video poker games.

Use strategy cards discreetly

It is not recommended that you take this Guide with you into a casino and use it while you play. 10/7 & 9/7 Double Bonus are covered in the Dancer/Daily Strategy Cards. These are durable six-sided cards that fit into a pocket or purse. The four levels of strategy presented in this Guide correspond closely to the levels on the strategy card. We recommend that you use these strategy cards discreetly.

Multi-line Games

In recent years, there has been the advent and growing popularity of multi-line or multi-play games such as Triple Play, Five Play, Ten Play, Fifty Play, and Hundred Play.[2] In these games, the initial five cards are dealt on the bottom line. Whatever the player holds on this bottom line is duplicated and shows up on all the other lines located higher on the screen. When the player presses DRAW, each line is completed from an identical but independent remaining pack of 47 cards. On Triple Play, it is as if the player has been dealt the same hand three times in succession and has held the same cards each time. The strategies for these multi-line games are IDENTICAL to those for their single-line counterparts with the same pay schedule.

---

[2] These multi-play machines are manufactured by International Game Technology, IGT, and are operated by casinos under license from Action Gaming Ltd.

Machines are fair

You may find this to be a leap of faith, but you can assume that video poker games are fair provided they are manufactured by the big American companies like IGT and Bally and are situated in the main U.S. gaming jurisdictions. You are playing against a sophisticated — yet fair — random number generator. However, although the cards that are dealt are purely random, you must expect the unexpected. A normal playing session does not produce paying combinations that actually occur exactly according to their average statistical frequency. Each hand that is dealt is totally independent of all hands that have gone before. It is sad but true that, even if you have never received a royal flush, you are no more or less likely to get one than if you have received one very recently. The consolation is that, after getting one royal flush, you are just as likely to get another one as you would have been if you had not received the first one. When selecting a machine in a given casino, the most important criterion by far is the pay schedule and denomination. When choosing between different casinos, the slot club and promotions are important. Once you have narrowed the search to the most lucrative machines within your budget, select on the basis of the comfort and speed of the machine, and environmental factors such as smoke, noise etc.

Taxes

The authors are strategists, not tax experts so be sure to check with your accountant. All U.S. residents are required to declare all gambling winnings. Whenever there is a payout on any video poker or other slot machine of $1,200 or more, a W2G form is issued with copies given to you and the IRS. If you are a dollar player and receive a $4,000 royal, you will be required to pay tax on this unless you have documented records of offsetting losses. Be sure to keep a detailed daily log of all your playing activity. Even if you receive no W2Gs within a year, winnings are still subject to tax. Foreign residents should be aware that people without U.S. identification and social security numbers normally have 30% of payouts of $1,200 or more withheld. There are some countries for whose residents this does not apply but be sure to check before playing.

Accuracy and avoiding silly mistakes

Knowing strategy is only one half of playing accurately. The other half is recognizing ALL the available options in a hand. The worst mistakes you can make are normally the silliest. For example, if you are dealt 3♣ K♦ K♥ 7♦ 3♠ and the machine "dings" to tell you that you have a paying hand, it is easy to notice immediately that you have the K♦ K♥ and miss the two pair, 3♣ K♦ K♥ 3♠. If, in a single hour-long playing session, you only once hold a single pair out of two pair, the expected loss from this mistake is far more than the expected gain from knowing and recognizing all the oddball situations presented in the Advanced Strategy.

In Double Bonus, recognizing all the hand options is often very much harder than it is in Jacks or Better. We mentioned earlier that you need to consider combinations that are never considered in Jacks or Better. For example, if you are dealt 5♥ A♣ 6♣ 2♦ 3♦, you would simply hold the A♣ in Jacks or Better and think nothing more about it. In Double Bonus, you not only need to know that any 4-card straight that includes an ace is better than the ace by itself, you also have to recognize its existence in the hand. 5♥ A♣ 2♦ 3♦ has significantly more value than the A♣ alone. However, what if you are dealt, 2♦ 3♣ 5♦ A♣ Q♣? Even if you know that the 4-card straight, 2♦ 3♣ 5♦ A♣, is less valuable than the A♣ Q♣, you need somehow to recognize that the hand also contains the 3-card flush, 3♣ A♣ Q♣, which, in this particular case, is preferable to both A♣ Q♣ and 2♦ 3♣ 5♦ A♣.

Unfortunately, you cannot train yourself "on the job" to spot all hand options. Knowing the strategy by heart helps, but the only way to be really sure is to practice on a computer using a program such as **Bob Dancer Presents WinPoker**. This will tell you when you make a mistake and will accumulate your score in terms of an accuracy percentage. When you make a mistake, you will be "beeped" and "flashed" that you have made an error. Eventually, you will learn not to miss a third flush card as in the above example.

Only play when at your best

Players who master the strategies in this Winner's Guide will have a small advantage over the casino. This advantage can easily be totally lost (and then some) if you play while tired, intoxicated, distracted, or otherwise not at your best. Having the discipline to play the game only when you at your very best is one attribute that separates winners from non-winners.

1.6. Strategy

1.6.1. How is preferred strategy determined?

There is a single criterion we use to determine strategy and that is the maximization of the statistical concept of expected return. Maximizing expected return does not mean that you will always find that, in hindsight, you will have made the best play if you look at the cards that appear on the re-deal. It means that, in the long run, the return on the game will be maximized. The strategy tables present a ranking of hand options that will achieve the highest expected value. In most video poker writings, "EV" is used to represent the expected value of a hand option assuming you play one coin and receive the full 800 coins per unit bet as the payout on the royal flush. We prefer to use the 5-coin expected return expressed in terms of dollars, "$EV." It is as if you are playing on a dollar denomination machine. We believe that expressing values in dollars and cents is easier for most people to understand. Whether we use single-coin EV or 5-coin $EV, the strategies are identical.

To illustrate this concept of maximizing expected return, consider the case in which you are dealt a 5-card flush that contains a 4-card royal flush, such as

K♣ Q♣ J♣ T♣ 6♣. The preferred play as given in all the strategies is to break the flush and hold the 4-card royal. However, the A♣ is the only card in the remaining 47-card pack that will yield the royal flush. Statistically, there is a 46 out of 47 chance that you will NOT get the royal. Of the seven clubs (not including the ace) left in the 47-card pack, the 9♣ will yield a straight flush, while the other six will mean that breaking the original paying flush will still result in a paying flush. In all the remaining 39 out of 47 cases, the result will be less than if you had held the flush. Nine out of 47 times you'll receive a high pair; six times you'll receive a straight; and in slightly more than half the cases (24 out of 47), you'll end up with nothing at all.

If you consider all the results that are possible and their likelihood, the expected return from holding the 4-card royal is almost three times as great as holding the paying flush. In the long term, the infrequent times that you will hit the royal will more than make up for all those times when you end up with less than the original paying flush.

Let us look at a hypothetical situation in which you, the reader, are sitting next to one of the authors who just happens to be looking at a paying flush that includes a K-high 4-card royal flush. This hand has a $EV of $99. If you were to offer us $98 for this hand, we would NOT sell it to you (assuming we could). We therefore obviously wouldn't dream of holding the $35 flush. If you were able to avoid uncertainty by selling every hand for only 1% less than its expected value, 10/7 would become a 99% game instead of a 100%+ game. The only way you can play the game and be a winner is to eke out the highest expected return on every hand you are dealt.

To be a winner, you must look at strategy from the point of view of long-term results. You must be playing within your means sufficiently such that you can ignore the short-term ups and downs. The preferred strategy is always that which achieves the highest expected return, independent of the risk. This does not mean that video poker winners do not take account of risk. It is critical for readers to understand that the decision concerning the level of risk is taken by the player when he chooses the particular game to be played, whether to play single-line or multi-line, and, most important of all, the denomination of play.

1.6.2. "Top down" strategy

Each strategy table begins with the instruction,

Select the hand option that appears highest in the following list:

For example, in the hand J♣ T♣ 7♣ 5♣ 5♦, you have the following four choices: a 4-card flush, J♣ T♣ 7♣ 5♣; a non-paying pair (or "low pair"), 5♣ 5♦; a 3-card straight flush, J♣ T♣ 7♣; and a 2-card royal flush, J♣ T♣. On all of the strategy tables, a 4-card flush is the first of these alternatives that you will come to when reading down the list of hand options. A low pair is found below this, followed by this type of 3-card straight flush, which is followed by this type of 2-card royal flush. The preferred strategy is to hold to J♣ T♣ 7♣ 5♣.

Because the most frequently occurring hand options are found in the lower ends of the strategy tables, many players read strategy tables from the bottom up. When doing it this way, the least preferred combination is arrived at first. We caution you that this can lead to mistakes if you do not continue reading up until all the hand options have been covered. For example, in the hand A♥ T♥ 9♣ 8♦ 5♦, a beginner may think that the alternatives are A♥ and A♥ T♥. If you read from the bottom up, you will quickly come to the ace. It would be wrong to think that this is the least preferred alternative and that A♥ T♥ is therefore superior. If you keep reading up, you will NOT come to a reference that covers A♥ T♥. This combination is never held in Double Bonus (or Jacks or Better). However, if you read from the top down, the first hand option you will come to will be the ace, confirming that this is the preferred combination. There is another type of potential problem that emerges in Level 4 when reading from the bottom up. Owing to oddball exceptions, there may be secondary references to a hand type in parentheses higher in the table.

1.6.3. The four levels of strategy

A special feature of these Winner's Guides (and also the Dancer/Daily Strategy Cards) is that the strategies are presented at four different levels of complexity from Level 1: "Beginner Strategy" to Level 4: "Advanced Strategy." (An exception to this is the game of Pick'em Poker, which only has a beginner and an advanced level.) The different strategy levels are designed to achieve the highest return in the long term for the level of complexity for which the player is comfortable.

The strategies for Double Bonus are more complicated than those of Jacks or Better. For example, Level 2 Double Bonus is at least as complicated as Level 3 Jacks or Better. It is perhaps as difficult to master Double Bonus if you already have Jacks or Better under your belt as it was to master Jacks or Better in the first place. If you are accustomed to playing Jacks or Better at the advanced level and understand the impact of penalty cards, you will no doubt aim to play Double Bonus at that level also.

Although Double Bonus is a difficult game to play well at an advanced level, the Beginner Strategy is relatively easy and even players who merely memorize and apply the General Principles in the Beginner Strategy would be able to play 10/7 Double Bonus even with the house, as long as the house offered cash back from the slot club of a quarter of a percent or so.

Level 2: "Recreational Strategy" is quite powerful and allows you to play 10/7 at approximately break-even. With any slot club at all, you are playing with an advantage while using this strategy. It is suitable for players who play, say, once a month, or perhaps two or three weekends a year. One beauty of the Level 1 and Level 2 strategy tables is that they are written in normal English. They use words rather than symbols and may therefore be less intimidating to the math-averse.

Level 3: "Basic Strategy" returns over 100.15% for 10/7 Double Bonus. This strategy is within the grasp of most motivated players. It is as high as many players will ever wish to get. There is a separate Basic Strategy for the game in which the straight flush pays 80 rather than 50. Great care has been taken in devising the Basic Strategies to ensure that the ranking of each general hand type takes account of the impact of any exceptions that are identified in Level 4. Basic Strategy is suitable for players who play frequently but who think that the intricacies of the Advanced Strategy are either too much of a headache to learn, or not worth the very small financial gain.

Level 4: "Advanced Strategy", returns the full 100.1725%. It is perfect. It is also very difficult to master. Assuming you are playing for dollars and can feed $3,000 per hour through the machine, the approximately 0.02% difference between Level 3 and Level 4 will add about 60¢ per hour to your return if you can play Level 4 at the same speed. Many players will conclude there is too little financial gain from the Advanced Strategy to be worth the effort it takes to master it.

Double Bonus can be particularly attractive when there is a promotion going on, such as double points or an extra bonus payout on a particular set of quads. During most promotions there is an implicit premium paid for speed. For players who can play Level 3 strategy significantly faster than they can play Level 4 strategy, it can make financial sense to stick with the lesser strategy. At the same time, most players who persist in the attempt to learn the Level 4 strategy find that, not only are they able to do so, they are also able over time to play this strategy quite fast. Playing Level 4 strategy fast is more lucrative than playing Level 3 strategy fast.

1.6.4. General Principles

We noted above how the game strategies are presented at four different levels of complexity. However, although the strategies change at each successive level, the discussion of the strategies is presented in terms of General Principles that do not change in any fundamental sense. Even if you are intent on reaching and playing at a high strategy level, you should not omit reading the chapters on the lower level strategies. For example, Level 1 identifies seven principles that are the most important principles of Double Bonus play. Level 2 identifies five additional principles, while Level 3 identifies an additional three.

If you have not played Double Bonus for some time or are switching to it from another game, review the General Principles. For convenience, there is a complete summary on pages 60-61. Even seasoned players who switch to Double Bonus from another game may be out of the habit of, for example, preferring consecutive 4-card straights to low pairs, or preferring 3-card flushes with no high cards to five new cards.

Although the principles remain fundamentally unchanged, the actual strategy tables change as you progress from Level 1 to Level 4. These strategy tables should be viewed as sources of reference. It is not recommended that you attempt to remember by heart the Beginner or Recreational Strategies. However, the more familiar you become with the principles, the better off you will be.

Chapter 2

Level 1: "Beginner Strategy"

2.1. Beginner Strategy Table (This applies to 10/7, 9/7, and 10/7/80.)

Select the hand option that appears highest in the following list:

1:	paying combinations of TWO PAIR or higher*	(e.g., A♣K♣Q♣J♣T♣; K♦Q♦J♦T♦9♦; 3♦3♠3♣3♥; 6♣6♦6♠3♣3♥; 4♣4♥4♦; 8♣8♦K♥K♦)
	except: break a FULL HOUSE for AAA	(e.g., from A♣4♣A♦4♠A♥, hold A♣A♦A♥)
	& break a FLUSH or STRAIGHT for a 4-card royal flush	(e.g., from A♠Q♠J♠T♠4♠, hold A♠Q♠J♠T♠; from A♣K♦Q♦J♦T♦, hold K♦Q♦J♦T♦)
2:	any 4-card straight flush	(e.g., A♥3♥4♥5♥; 8♠T♠J♠Q♠)
3:	HIGH PAIR [JJ – AA]	(e.g., J♥J♠; Q♥Q♣; K♣K♠; A♣A♦)
4:	4-card flush	(e.g., 2♣5♣8♣9♣; 6♥J♥Q♥K♥)
5:	3-card royal flush	(e.g., A♦K♦Q♦; K♠J♠T♠)
6:	consecutive 4-card straight [except A234]	(e.g., 4♥5♣6♥7♠; A♦K♣Q♣J♥)
7:	low pair [22 – TT]	(e.g., 4♥4♠; 9♦9♣)
8:	two suited high cards	(e.g., A♣J♣; K♦Q♦)
9:	any 3-card straight flush	(e.g., 4♥5♥6♥; 7♣T♣J♣)
10:	KQJ of different suits**	(e.g., K♦Q♣J♥)
11:	KQ, KJ or QJ of different suits**	(e.g., K♣J♥; Q♦J♣)
12:	K, Q or J [but not A] with suited T	(e.g., K♣T♣; Q♥T♥; J♠T♠)
13:	A***, K, Q, or J alone	
14:	If none of the above, draw five new cards.	

*   In 9/7 only, break two pair for a pair of aces. In all other cases, prefer two pair to a high pair.

**   When dealt three high cards of different suits of which one is an ace, discard the ace.

***   When an ace is accompanied by an unsuited high card or by a suited T, hold the ace alone.

NOTES:

A = ace; K = king; Q = queen; J = jack; T = 10.

Paying combinations are presented in capital letters.

"Any" means with or without gaps, and with or without high cards.

Always check the pay schedule to be sure the game has the highest return available.

The strategy is designed for maximum-coin play. As a general rule, always play maximum coins. However, if you are a first-timer, you may wish to play slowly and carefully with only a single-coin bet until you are confident in your ability to apply the strategy correctly.

2.2. Seven General Principles of Double Bonus Strategy

Those of you who are familiar with the Jack or Better Winner's Guide will find that there are some important differences in the Double Bonus General Principles and lower level strategies. These differences arise primarily from the 7 for 1 payout on the flush and the 5 for 1 payout on the straight. The following principles would be less suitable than the Jacks or Better principles on a Double Bonus game that paid 6 for 1 and 4 for 1 respectively.

Principle # 1

Hold all paying combinations of TWO PAIR or higher, except:

(a) **Break a FULL HOUSE only for AAA.**

(b) **Break a FLUSH or a STRAIGHT only for a 4-card-royal flush.**

(c) **Break TWO PAIR for a pair of aces in 9/7 only.**
At all other times, prefer TWO PAIR to one pair.

(a) In the Introduction, we emphasized the need always to hold the combination with the highest expected value, regardless of the variability there may be in the alternative outcomes. It is ironic that we are going to begin this discussion of strategy with a case in which it may be sensible for some players in some situations to hold a combination that does not have the greatest expected value.

In the hand A♥ A♠ A♣ 9♦ 9♠, holding the aces by themselves has a $EV of $50.57 (or $50.26 in 9/7) while holding all five cards is worth $50 (or only $45 in 9/7). There are players who like the guaranteed $50. Breaking the full house for the three aces gives only a 4% chance of receiving the fourth ace, a 6% chance or reconnecting on a full house, and a 90% chance of receiving only $15. In this situation, the authors always hold the aces since holding the full house is giving away 1% of the expected return. However, holding the full house is not a terrible play for occasional players, provided they are playing 10/7 and not 9/7.

Being dealt a full house can be one of bright spots of the playing session if you are playing a multi-line game. In "Hundred Play," holding all five cards gives you 100 sets of full houses. You have 5,000 coins "in the bank." However, if you hold the three aces, there are 100 lots of two spaces where you can pick up a fourth ace. Your statistical expectation is to get 4.25 sets of four aces. If you receive four, you are likely to get fairly close to 5,000 credits. If you get less than four, you are fairly certain of ending up with less than 5,000 credits. If you get five or more, you are GUARANTEED to end up with significantly more than 5,000 credits. On average, you will end up with 5,057 credits if you break the full house compared to 5,000 if you keep the full house – a nice few extra credits.

(b) If you are dealt a paying flush or straight, you have the option of a guaranteed $35 or $25 respectively. However, a 4-card royal flush that is A-high has an

$EV of around $93. When it is K-high, this rises to $99 owing to the additional possibility that it may end up as a KQJT9 straight or straight flush.

Although there is an overwhelming advantage to breaking a flush or a straight for a 4-card royal, you are going to end up with less than you invested more often than not. There is only one chance in 47 that you will receive the fifth card to the royal. When you break a flush for an A-high 4-card royal, there is a 57% chance that you will end up with nothing and an 83% chance that you will end up with less than a flush. However, we mentioned in the introduction that, if you were sitting next to one of the authors who just happened to be looking at a paying flush that included a 4-card royal flush, we would NOT sell it to you (assuming we could) for $1 less than its $EV, so we obviously wouldn't dream of holding a $35 flush.

We want you to be aware that Principle # 1 (b) does not say to break all paying combinations for a 4-card royal flush. There is one paying hand that should not be broken and that is a straight flush. There is only one straight flush that contains a 4-card royal flush and that is one that is K-high, such as K♥ Q♥ J♥ T♥ 9♥. Although the chance of being dealt a K-high straight flush is around one in 650,000, be sure to keep the guaranteed $250 rather than risk it on a 4-card royal that is "only" worth, in this case, around $95.

(c)   In Double Bonus, there is the same even-money payout on two pair as on a high pair. For this reason, many players find it tempting to break two pair for a high pair, particularly if the high pair is aces. After all, two pair can only be improved by becoming a full house, whereas a high pair has the possibility of the bonus payout on quads.

In 9/7, the $EV of a pair of aces is $8.77 versus $8.40 for two pair, so you always go for the aces. However, in 10/7, it is neck and neck with the two pair winning by a nose. Two pair is worth $8.83 while a pair of aces is worth $8.82. Although we understand the excitement of connecting on quad aces, there is only a 1 in 360 chance that a pair of aces will turn into quad aces. The 4 in 47 chance of turning two pair into a full house is worth more. In order for the authors to deviate from the rule of choosing the hand option with the highest $EV, there needs to be a factor such as avoiding down time and tipping due to hand pays. Both these factors would reinforce the worth of holding the two pair.

If you are playing fast and do not review the cards you are discarding before pressing DRAW, it can be easy to hold a high pair and miss a second pair. The "ding" made by the machine is the same whether it is a high pair or two pair. Face cards and aces are much easier to spot than low cards. It is a major mistake to hold a high pair and miss a second pair. A pair of Ks, Qs, or Js is worth only $7.29, compared to $8.83 for two pair. If you look at the hand Q♦ 5♣ Q♠ 3♦ 5♥, you may see how easy it can be to hold the Q♦ Q♠ as soon as it appears and miss the 5♣ 5♥. If you pause for just a moment after holding Q♦ Q♠ and look at the cards that you are about to discard, you will see the 5♣ 3♦ 5♥. This should prompt you into recognizing the second pair.

22

Principle # 2

Break a pair of aces only for a 4-card royal flush or a 4-card straight flush.

Most players will recognize when a pair of aces is accompanied by a 4-card royal flush, such as in the hand A♣ Q♣ A♦ J♣ T♣. Because a high pair only guarantees that you'll get your money back, few players are disturbed by breaking the high pair and going for the royal. Indeed, they WANT to go for the royal.

If you are dealt 3♣ A♣ A♥ 2♣ 5♣, it is a big surprise to most beginners that holding the four clubs is better than holding the aces – by a nearly 50% margin. Double Bonus players tend to be very attracted to aces and hold them whenever they get the chance. Not only are they guaranteed a minimum of the even money payout, there is also the chance that they may connect on quad aces. However, as we have mentioned before, there is only a 1 in 360 chance that a pair of aces will turn into quad aces. In contrast, the possibility of converting a 4-card straight flush, such as 3♣ A♣ 2♣ 5♣, into a paying straight flush is 1 in 47. A 1 in 360 chance of a $800 payout on quad aces is worth only $2.22, while a 1 in 47 chance of a $250 payout on a straight flush is worth $5.32. Together with the value of the secondary paying combinations, holding a pair of aces is worth $8.81 while holding the 4-card straight flush is worth $13.09

Principle # 3

The three combinations of {KK, QQ, JJ}, 4-card flush, and 3-card royal flush are preferable to all non-paying combinations except for a 4-card royal flush and a 4-card straight flush.

Stopgap Measure # 1

Until Level 3, prefer a HIGH PAIR to a 4-card flush. Prefer both to a 3-card royal flush.

In Jacks or Better, a high pair is always better than a 3-card royal flush, which itself is almost always better than a 4-card flush. Unfortunately, the situation is a lot more complex in Double Bonus. Although a pair of aces is always better than the other two options, there are many situations in which {KK, QQ, JJ} is inferior to a 3-card royal flush or a 4-card flush. Because two pair only pay even money rather than 2 for 1, {KK, QQ, JJ} is worth less in Double Bonus than in Jacks or Better. This is so despite the higher payout on quads and the higher payout on a full house in 10/7. While the value of {KK, QQ, JJ} is decreased, the value of a 4-card flush is increased significantly when the payout on the flush is raised from 6 to 7. Also the value of a 3-card royal flush is raised, but less significantly, by the higher payout on both the flush and the straight. The result of this is that these three options have ranges of values that overlap each other. Depending on the particular hand of which they are a part, there are important situations in which any one of the three can be of greater value than the other two.

Another problem with these three hand options is that it is possible for all three of them to be present in the same hand. Even when all three are present, there are situations in which any one of the three may be superior.

We are going to be spending a lot of time in this Guide talking about these three combinations. Apart from being inferior to the relatively rare 4-card royal flushes and 4-card straight flushes, they are more valuable than all other non-paying combinations. There are no exceptions to this.

Determining which of these three combinations is preferable is too complex to be covered at this level, or even at Level 2. It must wait until Level 3. Until that time, follow Stopgap Measure # 1 and prefer a high pair to a 4-card flush, and prefer both of these to a 3-card royal flush. This represents a major departure from Jacks or Better strategy. For example, if you are dealt A♣ Q♣ Q♥ T♣ 5♣, you have all three as options: the high pair, Q♣ Q♥; the 4-card flush, A♣ Q♣ T♣ 5♣; and the 3-card royal A♣ Q♣ T♣. Hold the high pair. If you are dealt a hand where there is no high pair but there is a 3-card royal contained within 4-card flush, hold the 4-card flush. For example, from K♥ J♥ T♥ 5♥ 3♣, prefer K♥ J♥ T♥ 5♥ to K♥ J♥ T♥.

Principle # 4

> **Prefer a consecutive 4-card straight (except A234) to a low pair. Prefer both to two suited high cards or any combination of high cards of mixed suits.**

There is a very important difference in strategy between Double Bonus and Jacks or Better arising from the 5 for 1 versus 4 for 1 payout on straights. In Double Bonus, all consecutive 4-card straights with the exception of A234 are ALWAYS more valuable than low pairs. This includes pairs of 2s, 3s, and 4s that have the possibility of becoming premium paying quads. In Jacks or Better, with the exception of KQJT being preferable to TT, low pairs are always more valuable than 4-card straights.

You will notice that consecutive 4-card straights are defined to exclude A234. The reason for this is that, except when a consecutive 4-card straight contains an ace, there are two ranks of cards that will complete it – one from above and one from below. However, A234 can only be completed from above. For example, 2345 can be completed with either an ace or a 6, while A234 can only be completed with a 5. Because AKQJ can only be completed from below, we would exclude it for the same reason as we exclude A234, except that it is not possible for a low pair to be in the same 5-card hand as AKQJ.

It is important to be on the lookout for consecutive 4-card straights when you have a low pair. This is not something you have to worry about in Jacks or Better. A 4-card straight is much easier to miss than a 4-card flush. For example, a fast or inattentive player who is dealt 6♦ 6♣ 4♣ 3♦ 5♣ may hold the 6♦ 6♣ and miss the fact that the hand also contains the more valuable 6♦ 4♣ 3♦ 5♣ (or 6♣ 4♣ 3♦ 5♣).

Principle # 5

Any 3-card straight flush should be extended into a 4-card flush or consecutive 4-card straight (except A234) when possible. Also, prefer a low pair to any 3-card straight flush.

This principle, like many of the others, implicitly assumes that there is no paying combination or higher-ranking combination also available. For example, in the hand J♣ J♦ T♦ 9♦ 8♣, the J♣ J♦ is clearly preferable to either J♦ T♦ 9♦ or J♣ T♦ 9♦ 8♣ (or J♦ T♦ 9♦ 8♣). Aside from this consideration, always extend a 3-card straight flush with any number of high cards or gaps into a 4-card flush or consecutive 4-card straight when an appropriate card is available.

In the hand Q♥ T♥ 9♥ J♣ 6♥, there is the 3-card straight flush, Q♥ T♥ 9♥, but there is also the 4-card flush, Q♥ T♥ 9♥ 6♥, and the consecutive 4-card straight, Q♥ T♥ 9♥ J♣. Both the flush and the straight are preferable to the 3-card straight flush. From Principle # 3, prefer the 4-card flush to the 4-card straight.

When a 3-card straight flush and a low pair occur in the same hand, as in T♦ 9♦ 7♦ 6♣ 6♥, hold the low pair even though it means giving up any possibility of obtaining a straight, a flush, or a straight flush. There is an important exception to this principle that is identified in Level 3.

There is a crucial distinction between a 3-card straight flush and a 3-card royal flush. In the Q♥ T♥ 9♥ J♣ 6♥ hand above, the Q♥ T♥ 9♥ is unquestionably a 3-card straight flush since it has no possibility of becoming a royal flush. However, even though a combination such as Q♣ J♣ T♣ has twice the possibility of becoming a straight flush (K♣ Q♣ J♣ T♣ 9♣ or Q♣ J♣ T♣ 9♣ 8♣) than a royal flush (A♣ K♣ Q♣ J♣ T♣), it must be classified as a higher-ranking 3-card royal flush. In live poker, a royal flush is a "special case" of a straight flush. This is not true in video poker where a royal flush is normally worth 4,000 while a straight flush is worth "only" 250 coins.

Principle # 6

Prefer two suited high cards to three high cards of mixed suits.

In the hand K♣ Q♦ J♣ 6♣ 4♥, the two suited high cards, K♣ J♣, are preferable to the three high cards of mixed suits, K♣ Q♦ J♣. When three unsuited high cards are held, there is a 44% chance of obtaining a high pair, but it is not possible to obtain any paying combination higher than a straight. When two suited high cards are held, the chance of obtaining a high pair is reduced to 30%, but ALL other paying combinations are also possible (except that when one of the suited high cards is an ace, no straight flush is possible). These added possibilities, particularly for getting a flush, make the two suited high cards preferable to three high cards of mixed suits. There are no exceptions to this principle at more advanced strategy levels. This is one of the most important principles of both Double Bonus and Jacks or Better.

Principle # 7

(a) When dealt three high cards of different suits of which one is an ace, discard the ace. When dealt KQJ of different suits, hold all three.

(b) Prefer two unsuited high cards to one, except, when one of the high cards is an ace, hold only the ace.

(c) When there is a single high card accompanied by a suited T, hold both the high card and the suited T when the high card is a K, Q or J. Discard the T when the high card is an ace.

(a)   Although the principle of discarding an ace from a combination of three high cards of different suits is common to both Jacks or Better and Double Bonus, it is one that is seldom followed by players who are playing by intuition rather than following a carefully crafted strategy. If one high card is good and two are better, then surely three are better still. This is true when the high cards are KQJ, but not true when one of the high cards is an ace. The problem with holding three high cards that include an ace is that it has the potential of becoming only a single straight, AKQJT. In contrast, KQJ has the potential of becoming AKQJT and KQJT9. This extra straight opportunity is enough to make the difference. There is a single exception to this principle that is identified in the Advanced Strategy, but it has very little financial significance.

In this Guide, we are normally approaching the principles of Double Bonus strategy from the starting point of Jacks or Better. However, we realize that some readers may be approaching Double Bonus from the standpoint of the popular game, "Double Double Bonus." In this game, quad aces pay 800 for a 5-coin bet, except this is raised to 2,000 when the fifth card (known as a kicker) is a 2, 3, or 4. When you are dealt three high cards of different suits of which one is an ace in Double Double Bonus, the preferred play is normally to hold the ace alone. It is important to note that, even though Double Bonus and Double Double Bonus have a similarity in their names, the strategies are very different indeed. Although the value of a solitary ace is significantly higher in Double Bonus than in Jacks or Better, it is always of less value than either two unsuited high cards without the ace, or all three high cards.

(b)   An important difference between the strategies for Double Bonus and Jacks or Better is that two unsuited high cards are ALWAYS better than one in Jacks or Better, but not always in Double Bonus. Because of the very high payout on quad aces, there is a general presumption in Double Bonus that an ace alone is preferable to an ace accompanied by another high card of a different suit. We will find in the Advanced Strategy that there are complex exceptions to this rule. However, at this stage, you are much better off if you always hold an ace alone instead of an unsuited AK, AQ, or AJ. In fact, there are many experienced and knowledgeable players who choose always to hold just the ace rather than spend the time working out whether the AK, AQ, or AJ would have been preferable. There are no exceptions to the rule that KQ, KJ, and QJ are preferable to a K, Q, or J alone.

(c)   There are four possible 2-card royal flushes that include a T. They are suited *AT*, *KT*, *QT*, and *JT*. The one with the lowest value is *AT*. This is due to the fact that the only straight that is possible when beginning with *AT* is AKQJT. Because of the low probability of completing a straight, an ace should never be accompanied solely by a suited T.

When beginning with *KT* suited, twice the number of straights are possible than when beginning with *AT* suited. You may end up with the equally likely AKQJT or KQJT9. In Jacks or Better, there are conditions under which it is better not to accompany a K with a suited T. There are no such conditions in Double Bonus.

The number of straight possibilities is increased further when it is a solitary Q that is accompanied by a suited T, and increased further still when it is a J. Suited *QT* and *JT* are always of more value than the Q or J alone. As the number of potential straights increases as you go from *AT* to *KT* to *QT* to *JT*, so too do the number of potential straight flushes. Interestingly, the contribution of potential straights to the expected returns is much larger than the contribution that comes from potential straight flushes.

Stopgap Measure # 2

Prefer two suited high cards to a 3-card straight flush, but prefer a 3-card straight flush to any combination of unsuited high cards or a single high card with suited T.

Three-card straight flushes tend to be difficult combinations in video poker. The main reason is the large number of combinations of high cards and gaps that are possible. For example, compare J♣ T♣ 9♣ with 8♠ 6♠ 4♠. The first has no gaps and a single high card; the second has two gaps and no high card. The value of the first one is approximately two thirds greater than the second. There are actually eight different combinations of the numbers of high cards and gaps that are possible.

Despite the variety of 3-card straight flushes, computer analysis shows that it is appropriate to hold 3-card straight flushes only in around 2% of all hands dealt. Because of their complexity and their infrequency, the Beginner Strategy makes the simplifying-yet-justifiable move of lumping them all together on line 9. Having them below two suited high cards is a stopgap measure as opposed to a basic principle. For as long as all 3-card straight flushes are grouped together, this is the best place to put them. However, we hope that the majority of readers will progress on to higher strategy levels in which the complexities and rankings of 3-card straight flushes will be progressively unraveled.

If you are dealt K♦ Q♦ 6♣ 7♣ 4♣, prefer the two suited high cards, K♦ Q♦, to the 3-card straight flush, 6♣ 7♣ 4♣, as per the rankings in the Beginner Strategy. However, if you are dealt J♣ T♣ 6♣ 7♣ 4♣, prefer the straight flush, 6♣ 7♣ 4♣, to the J♣ T♣. Although the Beginner Strategy table gives the '"correct" answer in both these two cases, there are other hands in which this stopgap positioning of 3-card straight flushes does not apply at higher strategy levels.

Stopgap Measure # 3

Prefer two unsuited high cards to a single high card with suited T.

In Principle # 7 (c) above, we saw that a single high card with suited T was of greatest value when the high card was a J, but reduced successively in value as we moved up to an ace. For similar reasons, two unsuited high cards are of greatest value when the higher of the two cards is a Q, and of least value when the higher card is an ace. Whether or not two unsuited high cards are preferable to a single high card with a suited T depends on which high cards one is talking about. However, as a general presumption, the two unsuited high cards are preferable, but this is only true when you limit your strategy to a one-size-fits-all rule. If you are dealt K♥ Q♦ T♥ 7♣ 5♣, hold K♥ Q♦ rather than K♥ T♥.

2.3. Beginner Strategy Examples

There now follows a set of examples of hands with explanations and answers. Following this, there is a practice set that is designed to see how you can do without help. These examples are an important adjunct to the examples that were presented when the General Principles were discussed. Many of the hands contain several alternative combinations and require an application of more than one principle. We want you to be aware that the most frequent mistakes that are made are not due to a misreading of the strategy table or the principles. Rather, they are due simply to missing one of the options contained in the hand.

The explanations of the answers will make reference to the General Principles whenever possible. The reason for this is that these seven General Principles hold true with only slight exceptions for all levels of strategy. They are not just for beginners. Together with other principles that will be added to them, they form the foundation of Double Bonus strategy.

Until you become familiar with the principles, you may find it necessary to read down the Beginner Strategy table to find the highest-ranking combination. However, although reading through the principles may take more time, such effort may help fix the General Principles in your mind and reduce the number of times that you will need to refer to the Beginner Strategy table. For example, the principle of preferring two suited high cards to three high cards of mixed suits is a principle of video poker that applies to most games where high pairs return even money. You will frequently be dealt hands in which it is relevant.

In contrast to the General Principles, it is NOT recommended that you try to memorize the Beginner Strategy table unless you have no intention of proceeding beyond Level 1. The Beginner Strategy table is a simplified reference source that will be modified at each subsequent level.

Whenever you are dealt a new hand, the first course of action is to identify all the alternative hand options. In most but not all cases, an application of one or more of the principles will quickly provide you with the correct answer. When you cannot find the answer from the principles, or when you wish to confirm your answer, refer to the Beginner Strategy table and find the hand option that is listed highest in the table.

The answers to all these questions are "correct" in the sense that they will not be reversed at higher strategy levels. These examples are in random order, and the order of the cards is deliberately jumbled in the way you would expect them frequently to be when playing in real life.

When there is a paying hand option present in the first five cards, it will normally be identified on the screen. We use parentheses following the five cards to show this.

1.   6♠ 6♥ K♣ Q♣ 3♦. Principle # 4 tells us that a low pair is preferable to two suited high cards. Prefer 6♠ 6♥ to K♣ Q♣. In a hand like this, you may sometimes see a player hold the K♣ Q♣ with an explanation of, "I like to go for royal flushes." They are entitled to do that, of course, but this is not equivalent to "I like vanilla ice cream better than chocolate." Any player who consistently chooses a second-best or third-best play cannot realistically expect to be a winner, whatever the reason may be .

2.   J♣ 8♦ 6♠ A♥ 9♣. In Jacks or Better, there are no exceptions to the rule that two high cards are better than one. However, in Double Bonus, Principle # 7 (b) tells us that, if there are two unsuited high cards of which one is an ace, hold only the ace. Prefer A♥ to J♣ A♥.

3.   A♣ 5♦ 3♣ K♣ Q♣. This hand includes the 4-card flush, A♣ 3♣ K♣ Q♣, and the 3-card royal flush, A♣ K♣ Q♣. Stopgap Measure # 1 tells us to prefer a 4-card flush to a 3-card royal. Hold A♣ 3♣ K♣ Q♣.

4.   A♣ K♣ K♦ A♥ A♠ (full house). Although this is an attractive looking full house with three aces and two Ks, the payout is the same on all full houses. Principle # 1 (a) instructs us to break a full house for three aces. Hold A♣ A♥ A♠ and hope that one of the cards that appears on the draw is the A♦.

5.   3♠ 4♠ 5♠ 6♥ 6♦. This hand contains: a 3-card straight flush, 3♠ 4♠ 5♠; a consecutive 4-card straight, 3♠ 4♠ 5♠ 6♥ (or 3♠ 4♠ 5♠ 6♦); and a low pair, 6♥ 6♦. Principle # 3 instructs us always to extend any 3-card straight flush into a 4-card flush or consecutive 4-card straight (except A234) when possible. It also informs us that a low pair is better than a 3-card straight flush. The competition in this hand is therefore between the 4-card straight and the low pair. The relationship between these two combinations is unequivocal in Double Bonus. As per Principle # 4, prefer a consecutive 4-card straight (except A234) to a low pair. Hold 3♠ 4♠ 5♠ 6♥ (or 3♠ 4♠ 5♠ 6♦).

6.   K♥ 9♥ Q♥ T♥ J♥ (straight flush). Our eyes light up when we are dealt a hand like this. Should we toss the 9 and go for the royal or keep the straight flush? There are four paying combinations that can accompany a 4-card royal, and they are a high pair, a straight, a flush, and a straight flush. Principles # 1 and 2 say to break the first three of these for a 4-card royal. They do not say to break a straight flush, so hold all five cards.

7.   K♥ Q♠ T♥ 7♦ 3♠. Stopgap Measure # 3 says to prefer two unsuited high cards to a single high card with suited T. Although it is "correct" that K♥ Q♠ is preferable to K♥ T♥, there are many exceptions in which a high card with suited T is preferable to two unsuited high cards. These will be revealed progressively at higher strategy levels.

8.   A♣ A♥ 3♥ 4♥ 5♥. Even though a straight flush only pays 250 while quad aces pay 800, Principle # 2 requires us to break a pair of aces for both a 4-card royal flush and a 4-card straight flush. Hold A♥ 3♥ 4♥ 5♥.

9.   K♠ Q♦ 8♣ 6♣ 5♣. The competition in this hand is between the two unsuited high cards, K♠ Q♦, and the 3-card straight flush, 8♣ 6♣ 5♣. We noted earlier that 3-card straight flushes tend to be difficult combinations in video poker owing to the large number of combinations of high cards and gaps that are possible. For the time being, we are working with Stopgap Measure # 2. This tells us to prefer a 3-card straight flush to any combination of unsuited high cards or a single high card with suited T. Prefer 8♣ 6♣ 5♣ to K♠ Q♦.

10.   A♥ Q♥ 7♥ 7♣ 5♥. This hand contains a 4-card flush, A♥ Q♥ 7♥ 5♥, and a low pair, 7♥ 7♣. Principle # 3 tells us to prefer the three combinations of high pair, 4-card flush, and 3-card royal flush to all non-paying combinations with the exception of 4-card royal flushes and 4-card straight flushes. Prefer A♥ Q♥ 7♥ 5♥ to 7♥ 7♣.

11.   K♠ K♥ 4♥ 3♦ 4♣ (two pair). If you hear the machine "ding" when it deals you these five cards and immediately notice the pair of Ks, you may think that you have a high pair. Whenever you see a high pair, be sure to check for a second pair in the hand. Even though a high pair and two pair have the same payout in Double Bonus after the draw, it is still a costly mistake to hold K♠ K♥ rather than K♠ K♥ 4♥ 4♣ before the draw.

12.   Q♦ J♠ T♦ 9♦ K♦ (straight). Although we will be told on the screen that this hand is a paying straight, it is hard not to be attracted to the 4-card straight flush, Q♦ T♦ 9♦ K♦. For as long as a straight flush pays "only" 250, there are no exceptions to Principle # 1 in which a straight should only be broken for a 4-card royal flush. In this hand, the certain return of 25 on the straight is better than uncertain return from holding the 4-card straight flush. Hold all five cards

13.   8♥ K♣ Q♥ J♥ T♥. It is very easy in this hand to spot the consecutive 4-card straight, K♣ Q♥ J♥ T♥, and the 3-card royal, Q♥ J♥ T♥, contained within it. We know by now that a 3-card royal is always preferable to a 4-card straight. However, this is not the correct play in this hand. After holding the Q♥ J♥ T♥, we hope you will notice that you

are about to discard an 8♥ that forms part of a 4-card straight flush with the Q♥ J♥ T♥. Hold 8♥ Q♥ J♥ T♥.

14.   A♣ Q♦ 8♥ 5♦ K♠. When we are dealt three high cards of different suits of which one is an ace, we know from Principle 7 (a) that we should discard the ace. Prefer Q♦ K♠ to A♣ Q♦ K♠.

15.   A♣ Q♦ J♣ 9♦ 5♥. Principle # 6 says to prefer two suited high cards to three high cards of mixed suits. When high cards are suited, it is possible to end up with a royal flush or "just" a regular flush (plus a straight flush when neither high card is an ace). None of these good things can happen when you hold unsuited high cards. A♣ J♣ is preferable to A♣ Q♦ J♣.

16.   A♣ 3♣ 3♦ A♥ 3♠ (full house). Although this full house contains aces, there are only two of them. Full houses should only ever be broken when there are three aces. Hold all five cards.

17.   J♠ A♠ 5♠ T♠ K♠ (flush). Here we have a paying flush that contains a 4-card royal. Holding the flush gives the certain return of $35, but this is considerably lower than the expected return from holding the 4-card royal of approximately $93. Some players hate to give up any "sure thing," and will keep all five cards. If this describes you, video poker is not the game for you. Principle # 1 says to break a paying flush for a 4-card royal flush. Throw away the 5♠ and go for the royal. Hold J♠ A♠ T♠ K♠.

18.   A♣ A♥ 6♣ 4♦ 4♠ (two pair). Principle # 1 (c) tells you to break two pair for a pair of aces if you are playing 9/7, but not if you are playing 10/7. However, the $EV from holding two pair in 10/7 is only one cent greater than from holding the pair of aces. This is one time when taking the gamble wouldn't cost you anything to speak of. When faced with this hand, the authors always hold the two pair.

19.   5♦ 7♦ 6♦ 8♠ A♦. This hand contains: the 3-card straight flush, 5♦ 7♦ 6♦; the consecutive 4-card straight, 5♦ 7♦ 6♦ 8♠; and the 4-card flush, 5♦ 7♦ 6♦ A♦. Principle # 3 places 4-card flushes together with high pairs and 3-card royals as superior to all non-paying combinations other than 4-card royal flushes and 4-card straight flushes. The 4-card flush is therefore more valuable than both the 4-card straight and the 3-card straight flush. Hold 5♦ 7♦ 6♦ A♦.

20.   5♦ 7♣ 8♣ T♥ A♥. From Principle # 7 (c), we know that a solitary high card should be accompanied by a suited T, except when the high card is an ace. Hold the A♥ without the accompanying T♥.

2.4. Beginner Strategy Practice Session

It is now time for you to test yourself to see whether you can recognize hand types and use the General Principles and Beginner Strategy table to determine the combination that is best to hold. When you are able to get all the answers correct, you are ready to proceed to Level 2: "Recreational Strategy." The numbers at the beginning of the lines indicate where the correct answers are to be found in the answer column. All answers are correct at all strategy levels for 10/7 and 9/7, and also for 10/7/80. You may wish to return to this practice session even after you have progressed well beyond Level 1.

Question						Answer				
17.	Q♠	9♥	J♠	T♠	8♠	1.	T♣	J♣	Q♣	8♣
4.	K♣	Q♦	A♣	T♣	J♣	2.	A♣		A♦	
20.	5♣	7♣	6♦	6♥	4♠	3.	K♣	A♣		
11.	T♦	9♣	Q♦	6♥	J♦	4.	K♣	A♣	T♣	J♣
16.	6♣	7♣	8♣	6♥	8♦	5.	A♦	5♦	3♦	
3.	K♣	Q♥	A♣	9♦	8♠	6.	J♣	6♣	A♣	T♣
19.	4♣	K♦	8♣	Q♠	6♣	7.	J♣	J♦		
10.	9♣	T♠	5♣	A♠	8♥	8.	T♣	9♣	J♦	8♠
1.	T♣	J♣	J♦	Q♣	8♣	9.	T♦	K♦		
12.	T♥	K♥	7♦	J♣	4♦	10.	A♠			
6.	J♣	6♣	A♣	T♦	T♣	11.	T♦	Q♦	J♦	
18.	7♣	9♣	Q♣	J♣	T♣	12.	K♥	J♣		
15.	8♣	Q♦	J♦	5♦	8♠	13.	2♠	4♠	3♠	K♠
2.	A♣	6♣	9♣	A♦	T♣	14.	draw 5 new cards			
8.	T♣	9♣	K♦	J♦	8♠	15.	8♣	8♠		
5.	Q♣	A♦	5♦	T♣	3♦	16.	6♣	8♣	6♥	8♦
13.	2♠	4♠	5♦	3♠	K♠	17.	Q♦	9♥	J♠	T♠ 8♠
7.	5♥	J♣	T♠	J♦	A♣	18.	7♣	9♣	Q♣	J♣ T♣
14.	3♥	5♥	T♠	9♠	7♦	19.	4♣	8♣	6♣	
9.	3♠	T♦	5♣	4♣	K♦	20.	5♣ 7♣ 6♦ 4♠ or 5♣ 7♣ 6♥ 4♠			

Chapter 3

Level 2: "Recreational Strategy"

3.1. Recreational Strategy Table (This applies to 10/7, 9/7, and 10/7/80.)

Select the hand option that appears highest in the following list:

1: paying combinations of TWO PAIR or higher except:
      break a FLUSH or STRAIGHT for a 4-card royal flush
    & break a FULL HOUSE for AAA

2: any 4-card straight flush

3: HIGH PAIR [JJ – AA]

4: 4-card flush

5: 3-card royal flush

6: consecutive 4-card straight [excluding A234]

7: low pair [22 – TT]

8: 3-card straight flush that is consecutive or has one or two high cards

9: 4-card straight with a gap that contains three high cards

10: *QJ* of the same suit

11: 3-card flush with two high cards

12: two suited high cards other than *QJ*

13: 3-card straight flush with one gap and no high cards

14: 4-card straight with a gap and one or two high cards (prefer two to one)

15: KQJ or QJT with the high cards of different suits

16: QJ unsuited, *JT* suited, or *QT* suited (always extend *QT* into a 3-card flush when possible)

17: 3-card straight flush with two gaps and no high cards

18: 3-card flush with one high card

19: KQ or KJ of different suits

20: A alone

21: *KT* of the same suit

22: K, Q, or J alone

23: 4-card straight with a gap and no high cards

24: 3-card flush with no high cards

25: If none of the above, draw five new cards.

Notes: (a) In 9/7 only, break two pair for a pair of aces. In all other cases, prefer two pair to a high pair.
    (b) Prefer a 4-card straight with a gap and one high card to the high card alone. When it has two or three high cards, prefer the inside straight except when all the high cards contained in the inside straight are of the same suit.
    (c) When dealt three high cards of different suits of which one is an A, discard the A.
    (d) When an ace is accompanied by an unsuited high card or a suited T, hold only the ace.

3.2. Continuation of General Principles

In the previous chapter on Beginner Strategy, we identified seven General Principles that apply to all variations of Double Bonus with payouts of 7 and 5 on a flush and straight respectively. Although there will be exceptions to some of these principles in more advanced strategies, these seven principles from a solid foundation for the more advanced strategies. In this section, we are going to add five additional principles. We'll be starting at number 8 to emphasize the fact that these are a continuation.

Principle # 8

(a) **Extend two suited high cards other than *QJ* into 3-card flushes when possible.**

(b) **Always prefer a 3-card flush including *QT* suited to the *QT* by itself. Prefer all other 3-card flushes with one high card to two unsuited high cards or a single high card with suited T, with the exception of the trio of combinations: QJ unsuited, *JT* suited, and *QT* suited.**

(a) One of the major differences between Double Bonus and Jacks or Better is that you never hold a 3-card flush in Jacks or Better unless it has the potential to become a straight flush or royal flush. With the payout on the flush at 7 rather than 6, things change. It is always better to extend two suited high cards that include an ace into a 3-card flush. This may seem mystifying to some. After all, from a 3-card flush that includes two high cards, there is no possibility of connecting on a royal, quads (including aces), full houses, or straights, and a much lower chance of 3-of-a-kind, two pair, or a high pair. However, the chance of connecting on the flush is approaching six times greater than if you do not extend into the 3-card flush.

There is also a general presumption that it is beneficial to extend two suited high cards in the form of *KQ* and *KJ* into a 3-card flush. However, it is never appropriate to extend *QJ* suited into a 3-card flush. The reason for the differences here is that, although 3-card flushes with two high cards all have the same value, suited *AK*, *AQ*, and *AJ* have less value than suited *KQ* and *KJ*, which themselves have less value than suited *QJ*. When two high cards include an ace, the only potential for a straight is AKQJT. With *KQ* and *KJ*, there is twice the possibility of obtaining a straight with the additional possibility of KQJT9, as well as the possibility of a *KQJT9* straight flush. With *QJ*, there is triple the possibility with the further addition of QJT98, plus an additional straight flush.

We will find in the Advanced Strategy that there is an important exception to extending suited *KQ* or *KJ* into a 3-card flush. However, if the choice is always extending into the 3-card flush or never extending, extend!

(b) This principle identifies an important difference in strategy when we are comparing *QT* suited to a 3-card flush of which it is part, versus *QT* suited to a 3-card flush of which it is not a part and which therefore is of another suit. When there is another card of the same suit as *QT* in the hand, the value of *QT* by itself is lowered because there is a lower chance that it will end up as a paying flush; the number of cards remaining in the pack of the same suit as *QT* has been reduced. In the absence of any higher-ranking combination, *QT* suited should always be extended into a 3-card flush when possible. We will see in later principles that any 3-card flush with one high card is always less valuable than a 4-card straight with a gap that contains at least one high card and also always less valuable than QJT.

Although *QT* suited is always of less value than a 3-card flush of which it is a part, it is normally of greater value than a 3-card flush with one high card of which it is not a part. For example, in the hand Q♣ T♣ 7♦ 5♣ 3♠, extend the Q♣ T♣ into Q♣ T♣ 5♣. However, in the hand K♠ Q♣ T♣ 7♠ 4♠, the 3-card flush with one high card, K♠ 7♠ 4♠, is of a different suit to Q♣ T♣, so prefer Q♣ T♣ to K♠ 7♠ 4♠.

Principles # 8 (a) and (b) are analogous. While the former refers to two suited high cards, the latter refers to two unsuited high cards. A 3-card flush with one high card is preferable to any two unsuited high cards other than QJ. In the same way that *QJ* suited is the most valuable of all the combinations of two suited high cards, QJ unsuited is the most valuable of all combinations of two unsuited high cards.

In line 16 of the Recreational Strategy table, there is a trio of hand types that will stay together on the strategy tables from here on. They are QJ unsuited, *JT* suited, and *QT* suited. What applies to QJ also normally applies to suited *JT* and *QT*. In general, each member of this trio has more value than a 3-card flush with one high card except in the conditions listed below:

1.   QJ unsuited is ALWAYS preferable to any 3-card flush with one high card.

2.   *JT* suited is ALWAYS preferable to a 3-card flush with one high card that doesn't include the *JT*. It is only in the Advanced Strategy that we will learn the few cases where a 3-card flush including *JT* is preferable to the *JT* by itself.

3.   A 3-card flush with one high card that includes *QT* suited is ALWAYS preferable to the *QT* by itself. *QT* suited is USUALLY preferable to a 3-card flush that doesn't include the *QT*. It is only in the Advanced Strategy that we will learn the few exceptions to this.

When there are three high cards of different suits in a hand in the form of AKQ or AKJ, we know from Principle # 7 (a) that it is better to drop the ace. In such situations, any 3-card flush is in competition with KQ or KJ. However, this 3-card flush may incorporate any one of the high cards including the ace. When three high cards of different suits are of the form AQJ, the QJ is always preferable to both the AQJ and any 3-card flush that may also be present. It is not surprising that, when there are three high cards of different suits in the form of KQJ, this combination has more value than any 3-card flush with one high card (or the unsuited QJ).

We will find in the Advanced Strategy that there is an important exception in which a 3-card flush with one high card has less value than KQ or KJ.

Here are some examples of Principles # 8 (a) and (b).

form A♠ K♦ Q♥ 6♠ 4♠	prefer A♠ 6♠ 4♠	to	K♦ Q♥	
from K♥ J♥ T♠ 8♥ 3♦	prefer K♥ J♥ 8♥	to	K♥ J♥	
from Q♥ J♥ T♠ 7♥ 4♦	prefer Q♥ J♥	to	Q♥ J♥ 7♥	
form A♠ K♦ Q♥ 6♠ 4♠	prefer A♠ 6♠ 4♠	to	K♦ Q♥	
from K♣ J♦ 9♦ 6♦ 2♠	prefer J♦ 9♦ 6♦	to	K♣ J♦	
from A♥ Q♦ J♠ 7♦ 5♦	prefer Q♦ J♠	to	Q♦ 7♦ 5♦	
from A♠ Q♥ J♣ 8♠ 2♠	prefer Q♥ J♣	to	A♠ 8♠ 2♠	
from K♣ J♦ T♦ 5♦ 2♥	prefer J♦ T♦	to	J♦ T♦ 5♦ or K♣ J♦	
from A♣ Q♥ T♥ 7♣ 6♣	prefer Q♥ T♥	to	A♣ 7♣ 6♣	
from K♦ Q♣ T♣ 7♥ 5♣	prefer Q♣ T♣ 5♣	to	Q♣ T♣ or K♦ Q♣	
from K♣ Q♥ J♠ 6♣ 4♣	prefer K♣ Q♥ J♠	to	Q♥ J♠ or K♣ 6♣ 4♣	

Principle # 9

(a) **Always prefer a 4-card open-ended straight to a 4-card inside straight.**

(b) **When a 4-card inside straight has two or three high cards, prefer the inside straight to the high cards except when all the high cards in the inside straight are of the same suit.**

(c) **When two 4-card inside straights occur in the same hand, prefer the one with the extra high card, if any.**

The term "open-ended straight" refers to any consecutive 4-card straight that can be completed both from above and below. The only consecutive 4-card straights that cannot be completed from above and below are the ones containing an ace, namely A234 and AKQJ.

The term "inside straight" refers to any 4-card straight for which one and only one card can be used to complete it. Any 4-card straight with a gap is an inside straight, as are A234 and AKQJ. When we use the terms "open-ended straight" and "inside straight" in Double Bonus, we are ALWAYS referring to 4-card combinations.

In Double Bonus, straights pay 5 for 1 versus only 4 for 1 in Jacks or Better. For this reason, we hold 4-card straights considerably more often in Double Bonus. In Jacks or Better, a 4-card inside straight must have a minimum of three high cards before it is eligible to be held. In Double Bonus, there are situations in which inside straights with any number of high cards may be held. We will see later that it is even appropriate in Double Bonus to prefer an inside straight with one high card to the high card alone.

(a)   It is possible for both a 4-card inside straight and a 4-card open-ended straight to occur in the same hand. For example, in the hand A♣ Q♦ J♥ T♣ 9♦, we have the inside straight with three high cards, A♣ Q♦ J♥ T♣, and the open-ended straight with two high cards, Q♦ J♥ T♣ 9♦. Even though there is an extra high card in this inside straight, this does not offset the fact that this straight can only be completed with a K. It has considerably less value than the open-ended straight for which there are cards of two ranks, Ks or 8s, that will complete it.

(b)   In Jacks or Better, two suited high cards are always preferable to a 4-card inside straight with three high cards. For example, from K♣ Q♣ J♦ 9♥ 7♦, the K♣ Q♣ would be preferred to the K♣ Q♣ J♦ 9♥. In Double Bonus, the inside straight is preferable unless ALL the high cards contained in the straight are of the same suit. Since the KQJ are of mixed suits, prefer K♣ Q♣ J♦ 9♥ to K♣ Q♣ in Double Bonus. In contrast, from K♣ Q♣ T♦ 9♥ 7♦, hold K♣ Q♣ rather than K♣ Q♣ T♦ 9♥ because the high cards are suited. Note that this condition refers to the high cards contained within the inside straight. In the hand A♥ Q♦ J♦ 9♣ 8♣, the high cards contained in the inside straight are suited, even though all the high cards in the hand are not suited. Because the unsuited A♥ is not contained within the straight, prefer Q♦ J♦ to Q♦ J♦ 9♣ 8♣.

(c)   When two 4-card inside straights occur in the same hand, one of them will frequently have an extra high card. For example, in Q♣ T♦ 9♥ 8♥ 6♦, the alternatives are Q♣ T♦ 9♥ 8♥ and T♦ 9♥ 8♥ 6♦. Since the first of these has one high card while the second has no high cards, hold Q♣ T♦ 9♥ 8♥. Similarly, from K♥ J♦ T♣ 9♣ 7♣, prefer K♥ J♦ T♣ 9♣ with two high cards to J♦ T♣ 9♣ 7♣ with one high card. It is not possible for two inside straights to have the same number of high cards except when this number is zero. In the hand 3♣ 4♦ 6♣ 7♥ 8♣, both 3♣ 4♦ 6♣ 7♥ and 4♦ 6♣ 7♥ 8♣ have no high cards and are of equal value. Hold whichever one you wish.

Principle # 10

    (a)   Prefer QJT to: QJ unsuited, *QT* suited, *JT* suited, or any 3-card flush with one high card. However, prefer QJT8 to QJT.

    (b)   Prefer suited *QT* and *JT* to unsuited KQ or KJ, and also to an ace alone.

(a) Unsuited QJT is a combination that is never held in Jacks or Better. However, with the straight paying 5 rather than 4 in Double Bonus, QJT is always preferable to unsuited QJ, or suited *QT* or *JT*. For example, from Q♦ J♣ T♣ 7♦ 4♠, prefer Q♦ J♣ T♣ to Q♦ J♣ or J♣ T♣. However, in the hand Q♠ J♠ T♦ 7♦ 3♣, the Q and J are suited, so prefer Q♠ J♠ to Q♠ J♠ T♦.

Unsuited QJT is also preferable to any 3-card flush with one high card. For example, in the hand Q♥ T♥ J♦ 5♥ 3♣, prefer Q♥ T♥ J♦ to Q♥ J♦ or Q♥ T♥ 5♥.

From Principle # 9 (b), we know that a 4-card inside straight with two unsuited high cards is preferable to the high cards alone. When you see QJT in a hand, always check whether there is an 8 (or, of course, a 9) to accompany it. In the hand Q♣ J♦ T♦ 8♥ 5♠, prefer Q♣ J♦ T♦ 8♥ to Q♣ J♦ T♦. However, in the hand Q♥ J♥ T♠ 8♣ 3♦, the two suited high cards, Q♥ J♥, are preferable to both Q♥ J♥ T♠ 8♣ and Q♥ J♥ T♠.

(b)   In Jacks or Better, there is a complicated relationship between two unsuited high cards and a single high card with suited T. Fortunately, this relationship is somewhat easier in Double Bonus. The higher payout on the flush and the straight increase the return on a high card with suited T by far more than they increase the return on two unsuited high cards. *QT* suited and *JT* suited are both always more valuable than unsuited KQ or KJ, and also more valuable than an ace by itself.

Principle # 11

(a)   **Always extend a 2-card royal flush or single high card into a 3-card or 4-card straight flush when possible.**

(b)   **Prefer a consecutive 3-card straight flush (except *A23* and *234*) to two suited high cards, or any combination of unsuited high cards, or any inside straight.**

(c)   **Prefer a 3-card straight flush with one gap to any combination of unsuited high cards or any inside straight.**

(d)   **A 3-card straight flush with two gaps and no high cards is more valuable than a 4-card inside straight with no high cards, but less valuable than an inside straight with one or two high cards.**

(e)   **Prefer a 3-card straight flush with two gaps and no high cards to a single high card, a single high card with suited T, or two unsuited high cards except for the three combinations: QJ unsuited, *QT* suited, and *JT* suited.**

(a)   In both Jacks or Better and Double Bonus, there are no exceptions to the principle that you should ALWAYS extend a 2-card royal flush or single high card into a 3-card or 4-card straight flush when possible. Although adding a straight flush card eliminates the possibility of getting a royal, it should always be done.

Two-card royal flushes include any two suited high cards, and a single high card with a suited T. For example, in the hand K♣ Q♣ 9♣ 7♦ 6♠, the K♣ Q♣ 9♣ has significantly more valuable than the K♣ Q♣ by itself. When a hand contains, say, Q♦ J♦ or Q♦ T♦, always look to see if there is a 9♦ and/or an 8♦ to accompany it (in the case of Q♦ T♦, also look for any lower diamond that would make up a 3-card flush with one high card). If you are dealt J♠ T♠, remember that you can upgrade it with a 9♠, 8♠, or 7♠. These straight flush cards are sometimes easy to miss.

When a hand contains a single high card in the form of an ace, it can be easy to miss the possibility of extending it into a 3-card straight flush. For example, in the hand 2♥ 6♦ A♥ J♠ 5♥, it is easy to focus on whether to hold the A♥ J♠ or just the A♥ and miss the 2♥ A♥ 5♥.

It is very important to remember that this principle like most of the others assumes that there are no higher-ranking combinations available. For example, in the hand K♠ Q♣ J♦ T♦ 7♦, the J♦ T♦ 7♦ has more value than J♦ T♦ but has considerably less value than the open-ended straight, K♠ Q♣ J♦ T♦.

(b)   When a 3-card straight flush is consecutive, there are normally three alternative straights and straight flushes that it may turn into. For example, 7♠ 8♠ 9♠ may become 56789, 6789T, or 789TJ. There are two consecutive 3-card straight flushes that do not fit into this category, and they are *A23* (which may turn into only one straight or straight flush) and *234* (which may turn into two). These two combinations will be discussed in greater detail in Level 3.

As in Jacks or Better, consecutive 3-card straight flushes are ranked above that of two suited high cards. Remembering Principle # 5, the only non-paying combinations that are preferable to a consecutive 3-card straight flush are a 4-card flush, an open-ended 4-card straight, and a low pair.

Examples of Principle # 11(b):

from 8♦ 9♦ T♦ Q♣ K♣	prefer 8♦ 9♦ T♦	to	Q♣ K♣
from 9♣ T♣ J♣ K♦ A♥	prefer 9♣ T♣ J♣	to	T♣ J♣ K♦ A♥

However, remember that:

from 4♣ 5♣ 6♣ 8♦ 8♥	prefer 8♦ 8♥	to	4♣ 5♣ 6♣
from 6♥ 7♥ 8♥ 9♦ J♦	prefer 6♥ 7♥ 8♥ 9♦	to	6♥ 7♥ 8♥
from 2♠ 9♠ T♠ J♠ K♣	prefer 2♠ 9♠ T♠ J♠	to	9♠ T♠ J♠

It is sometimes easy to miss all the alternatives that are present in a hand. For example, consider the hand J♦ K♦ 8♥ 9♥ T♥. This is a hand where many an experienced player may make a mistake. At first glance, it would seem as though the alternatives are J♦ K♦ and 8♥ 9♥ T♥. However, hiding within this hand is the 4-card open-ended straight, J♦ 8♥ 9♥ T♥. Principle # 5 says to prefer an open-ended straight to any 3-card straight flush. J♦ 8♥ 9♥ T♥ is preferable to both J♦ K♦ and 6♥ 7♥ 8♥.

(c)   When a 3-card straight flush has a single gap (except for *A24* and *A34*), there are only two alternative straights and straight flushes that it can end up as compared to three when it is consecutive. For example, 2♥ 4♥ 5♥ can become A2345 and 23456, while 3♦ 4♦ 5♦ can become A2345, 23456, and 34567. This lowers the ranking in the strategy table to below two suited high cards, but above any combination of unsuited high cards or any 4-card inside straight.

Examples of Principle # 11(c):

from 4♣ 5♣ 7♣ 9♦ K♥	prefer 4♣ 5♣ 7♣	to	K♥
from 2♦ 3♦ 5♦ Q♣ T♣	prefer 2♦ 3♦ 5♦	to	Q♣ T♣
from 3♥ 5♥ 6♥ J♠ A♣	prefer 3♥ 5♥ 6♥	to	A♣ or J♠ A♣
from 8♣ 6♣ 9♣ J♠ Q♥	prefer 8♣ 6♣ 9♣	to	8♣ 9♠ J♠ Q♥
from 5♥ 7♥ 8♥ Q♦ A♦	prefer Q♦ A♦	to	5♥ 7♥ 8♥

(d)   One of the easy features to remember of all variations of Jacks or Better is that a 3-card straight flush with two gaps and no high cards should only be held if there is absolutely nothing else worth holding. There is never any difficulty knowing what to do with it. Unfortunately, things are very much more complicated in Double Bonus where the extra payouts on the both the flush and the straight raise this type of straight flush from off the bottom of the strategy table.

A 3-card straight flush with two gaps and no high cards is always more valuable than a 4-card inside straight with no high cards, but always less valuable than one with one or two high cards (there is an exception to this when the straight flush pays 80 rather than 50). For example,

from 3♣ 5♦ 6♣ 7♣ T♣	prefer 3♣ 6♣ 7♣	to 3♣ 5♦ 6♣ 7♣
from A♥ 2♦ 4♠ 5♠ 8♠	prefer A♥ 2♦ 4♠ 5♠	to 4♠ 5♠ 8♠.

(e)   If you combine the categories of two unsuited high cards and a single high card with suited T, there is a trio of combinations that stand out as being of most value and are generally ranked together in Double Bonus. This trio is comprised of QJ unsuited, *JT* suited, and *QT* suited. These combinations are always more valuable than a 3-card straight flush with two gaps and no high cards (there is an exception to this only when the straight flush pays 80 rather than 50). Apart from these three combinations, prefer a 3-card straight flush with two gaps and no high cards to a single high card, a single high card with suited T, or two unsuited high cards. We will find in the Advanced Strategy that there are some oddball cases in which this type of straight flush has less value than an A or J alone.

Principle # 12

(a)   **Extend a single high card or high card with suited T into a 4-card inside straight or a 3-card flush when possible; prefer the inside straight to the 3-card flush.**

(b)   **Hold a 4-card inside straight with no high cards, or a 3-card flush with no high cards, only if there is absolutely nothing else in the hand worth holding; prefer the inside straight to the 3-card flush.**

40

(a)   4-card inside straights with one high card and 3-card flushes with one high card are held in almost no other game of video poker. The reason they are held in Double Bonus is because of the high payouts on straights and flushes. Video poker players who are seasoned in other games are cautioned to be on the lookout for these combinations.

In a hand such as J♠ T♠ 8♦ 7♦ 3♠, holding J♠ T♠ 8♦ 7♦ is preferable to either J♠ T♠ or J♠ T♠ 3♠. This is somewhat remarkable since J♠ T♠ would be the correct play in every other video poker game we have studied. Equally remarkable is that, from A♥ 9♥ 5♦ 3♠ 2♥, the correct play is A♥ 5♦ 3♠ 2♥. Holding the ace by itself would be the play of most beginners, but is the third-best play in this hand, where it is also worth less than A♥ 9♥ 2♥. Notice that in both these examples, there is a 3-card flush with one high card and a 4-card inside straight with one high card occurring in the same hand, and where going for the inside straight is the better play.

(b)   A hand that looks very similar to J♠ T♠ 8♦ 7♦ 3♠ above is Q♦ T♦ 9♠ 7♥ 6♦. They both contain a single high card with suited T, a 4-card inside straight, and a 3-card flush with one high card. However, there is a very important difference. In the second example, the inside straight, T♦ 9♠ 7♥ 6♦, contains no high cards. Principle # 12 (b) says that a 4-card inside straight with no high cards and a 3-card flush with no high cards should only be held if there is absolutely nothing else in the hand worth holding. The T♦ 9♠ 7♥ 6♦ has less value than the Q♦ T♦. However, we know from Principle # 12 (a) that the 3-card flush, Q♦ T♦ 6♦, has more value than the Q♦ T♦ alone. By implication, a 3-card flush with one high card, such as Q♦ T♦ 6♦, is always preferable to an inside straight with no high cards, such as T♦ 9♠ 7♥ 6♦.

The hand 3♣ 5♦ 6♠ 7♣ T♣ contains both a 4-card inside straight with no high cards, 3♣ 5♦ 6♠ 7♣, and a 3-card flush with no high cards, 3♣ 7♣ T♣. Although these are bottom-of-the-barrel combinations, they are both better than throwing all five cards away. In the absence of any high cards, an inside straight is always superior to a 3-card flush.

3.3. Recreational Strategy Examples

These examples are in random order, and the order of the cards is deliberately jumbled as they frequently may be when playing in real life. Wherever possible, the preferred plays are arrived at by an application of one or more of the General Principles.

1.   A♥ Q♠ 6♥ T♠ 4♥. The alternatives in this hand are the Q♠ T♠ and the 3-card flush with one high card, A♥ 6♥ 4♥. Although we know that *QT* suited always has less value than a 3-card flush of which it is a part, it is generally more valuable than a 3-card flush with one high card of a different suit, as per Principle # 8 (b). Prefer Q♠ T♠ to A♥ 6♥ 4♥.

2.   7♣ 5♣ T♣ 9♦ 6♠. This hand contains a 4-card inside straight with no high cards, 7♣ 5♣ 9♦ 6♠ (or 7♣ T♣ 9♦ 6♠), and a 3-card flush with no high cards, 7♣ 5♣ T♣.

These are the two lowest-ranking combinations in Double Bonus and should only be held when there is absolutely nothing else worth holding. Principle # 12 (b) instructs us to prefer the inside straight to the 3-card flush in this situation. Hold 7♣ 5♣ 9♦ 6♠ or 7♣ T♣ 9♦ 6♠, it doesn't matter which.

3. J♦ K♦ T♣ 8♣ 9♦. There are several alternatives in this hand and it is easy to make a mistake. If you forget the strategy rankings, it is always possible to look them up in this Guide or on the Dancer/Daily Strategy Card. However, if you miss one the alternative hand options, you may be sunk without knowing it. When a hand like this appears on the screen, the two suited high cards, J♦ K♦, are likely to gain your attention immediately. Even though J♦ K♦ may feel like a good combination to hold, you must ask yourself whether there is anything that should be added to it, or anything that is altogether better. On closer examination, you may notice the 4-card inside straight with two high cards, J♦ K♦ T♣ 9♦. However, because the two high cards in this inside straight are suited, the high cards alone are more valuable than the inside straight. Harder to spot in this hand is the fact that these two suited high cards can be extended into the 3-card straight flush, J♦ K♦ 9♦ – but even this is the wrong answer. Hopefully, before you are fed up with looking at this hand, you will have noticed that there is also a 4-card open-ended straight, J♦ T♣ 8♣ 9♦. Principles # 4 and 5 are bedrocks of Double Bonus strategy and tell us that an open-ended straight is preferable to two suited high cards and any 3-card straight flush. Hold J♦ T♣ 8♣ 9♦.

4. A♥ K♣ Q♣ T♣ 5♣. From Principle # 3, we know that high pairs, 3-card royals, and 4-card flushes are preferable to all non-paying combinations other than 4-card royals and 4-card straight flushes. Both K♣ Q♣ T♣ and K♣ Q♣ T♣ 5♣ have more value than the inside straight, A♥ K♣ Q♣ T♣. If you are familiar with Jacks or Better strategy, the 4-card flush, K♣ Q♣ T♣ 5♣, may look like an unlikely combination. However, until Level 3, we are still working with Stopgap Measure # 1 in which a 4-card flush should be held in preference to a 3-card royal. Prefer K♣ Q♣ T♣ 5♣ to K♣ Q♣ T♣.

5. Q♥ J♥ T♥ 9♠ 9♣. This hand contains: the 3-card royal flush, Q♥ J♥ T♥; the open-ended straight, Q♥ J♥ T♥ 9♠ (or Q♥ J♥ T♥ 9♣); and the low pair, 9♠ 9♣. Although 4-card open-ended straights are always preferable to low pairs in Double Bonus, they have significantly less value than 3-card royals. Hold Q♥ J♥ T♥.

6. J♣ 3♣ 8♣ 9♦ 7♠. In Jacks or Better, the J♣ is the only eligible alternative from this hand. However, in Double Bonus, all 3-card flushes and 4-card inside straights are also eligible for consideration. In this hand, the J♣ is competing with the 3-card flush, J♣ 3♣ 8♣, and the inside straight, J♣ 8♣ 9♦ 7♠. Principle # 12 (a) says that a single high card should be extended into a 4-card inside straight or a 3-card flush when possible. Both J♣ 3♣ 8♣ and J♣ 8♣ 9♦ 7♠ are more valuable than the J♣ alone. This principle also says to prefer the inside straight to the 3-card flush. Hold J♣ 8♣ 9♦ 7♠.

7. T♣ Q♣ K♥ 2♦ 5♣. It is important to notice that this hand contains the 3-card flush with one high card, T♣ Q♣ 5♣, as well as the two unsuited high cards, Q♣ K♥, and the high card with suited ten, T♣ Q♣. We know from Principle # 10 (b) that T♣ Q♣ is more valuable than Q♣ K♥. However, Principle 8 (b) tells us that *QT* suited has less

value than a 3-card flush of which it is part. There is no exception to this part of the principle even in the Advanced Strategy. Because there is the 5♣ to go along with the T♣ Q♣, prefer T♣ 5♣ Q♣ to both T♣ Q♣ and Q♣ K♥.

8. K♠ Q♥ 3♣ 4♣ 7♣. A 3-card straight flush with two gaps and no high cards is the lowest-valued combination that is ever held in Jacks or Better. In Double Bonus, there are several combinations that are worth less. Why is there this difference when the straight flush is equally hard to get in both games and is worth the same amount? The answer is that, although you may be aiming for a straight flush, you will get a regular flush or a regular straight considerably more often than a straight flush. Both flushes and straights pay more in Double Bonus than they do in Jacks or Better. From Principle # 11 (e), we know that this least valuable of all 3-card straight flushes is more valuable than a single high card, a single high card with suited T, or two unsuited high cards with the exception of the trio of combinations: QJ unsuited, *JT* suited, and *QT* suited. Although there are some oddball exceptions to this principle in the Advanced Strategy, these do not include any related to KQ or KJ. Prefer 3♣ 4♣ 7♣ to K♠ Q♥.

9. J♣ A♦ 6♠ 5♠ T♣. Principle # 7 (b) tells us that an ace is generally of more value alone than when accompanied by another high card of a different suit. At this level, the J♣ A♦ combination is not a consideration in this hand. The competition is between the A♦ and the J♣ T♣. Principle # 10 (b) says to prefer J♣ T♣ to A♦.

10. A♠ K♣ J♥ 4♠ 6♠. Experienced players who know strategy by heart often make mistakes without realizing it. It is only when they practice on a computer with a program such as *Bob Dancer Presents WinPoker* that they can find out just how accurately or inaccurately they are playing. If you are playing fast and are dealt this hand, you may immediately look at A♠ K♣ J♥ and decide that you need to drop the ace and hold just the K♣ J♥. However, if you follow the practice of reviewing the cards that are going to be discarded before pressing DRAW, you will see that you are about to discard A♠ 4♠ 6♠. On the Recreational Strategy table, A♠ 4♠ 6♠ is covered by line 18, while K♣ J♥ is covered on line 19. A♠ 4♠ 6♠ has more value than K♣ J♥.

11. T♠ 9♦ 8♣ 6♣ Q♦. If you study this hand, you will find that, as well as containing the 4-card inside straight with no high cards, T♠ 9♦ 8♣ 6♣, it also contains the 4-card inside straight with one high card, T♠ 9♦ 8♣ Q♦. When two inside straights occur in the same hand, Principle # 9 (c) instructs us to prefer the one with the extra high card if any. Prefer T♠ 9♦ 8♣ Q♦ to T♠ 9♦ 8♣ 6♣.

12. 3♦ J♣ A♦ 7♥ K♦. We know from Principle # 6 that two suited high cards are always preferable to three high cards of mixed suits. A♦ K♦ has more value than J♣ A♦ K♦. However, Principle # 8 (a) says that two suited high cards other than *QJ* should be extended into 3-card flushes when possible. Hold 3♦ A♦ K♦ rather than A♦ K♦.

13. Q♣ J♦ 6♣ 8♥ T♣. If you were dealt this hand in Jacks or Better, you would hold Q♣ J♦ and be done with it. However, this hand is a lot more complicated in Double Bonus. First, we know from Principle # 10 (a) that Q♣ J♦ T♣ is preferable to Q♣ J♦,

Q♣ T♣, and Q♣ T♣ 6♣. However, this principle recognizes the need always to check whether there is an 8 to add to QJT to make up a higher-ranking 4-card inside straight with two high cards. In this hand, prefer Q♣ J♦ 8♥ T♣ to Q♣ J♦ T♣.

14.　8♥ 9♣ 7♣ J♥ Q♥. There are many alternatives in this hand. There are two 4-card inside straights, 8♥ 9♣ 7♣ J♥ and 8♥ 9♣ J♥ Q♥. Since the first of these has one high card while the second has two, you would hold the second one – if there weren't better alternatives. Principle # 9 (b) says to prefer an inside straight with two high cards to the high cards alone provided the high cards are not suited. Since the J♥ Q♥ are suited, they are more valuable by themselves than in the combination 8♥ 9♣ J♥ Q♥. This is not the end of the story though. It is easy in this hand to miss the fact that the 8♥ forms part of a potential straight flush with J♥ Q♥. Principle # 11 (a) says that you should ALWAYS extend 2-card royal flushes such as J♥ Q♥ into 3-card or 4-card straight flushes when possible. The ranking of alternatives in this hand is therefore: first, 8♥ J♥ Q♥; second, J♥ Q♥; third, 8♥ 9♣ J♥ Q♥; and fourth, 8♥ 9♣ 7♣ J♥.

15.　9♥ 3♠ K♣ Q♦ J♦. At first glance, this looks like an easy comparison in which the two suited high cards, Q♦ J♦, are preferable to the three high cards of mixed suits, K♣ Q♦ J♦. If your initial response is to hold Q♦ J♦, be sure to review the cards you are about to discard and you will see that they are 9♥ 3♠ K♣. Perhaps this review will prompt you into seeing that there is also a 4-card inside straight with three high cards, 9♥ K♣ Q♦ J♦. Principle # 9 (b) tells us that a 4-card inside straight with two or three high cards is preferable to the high cards alone when not all of the high cards contained in the straight are of the same suit. When you have two suited high cards in a hand, extend them into a 4-card inside straight if you are able to include an additional high card. Prefer 9♥ K♣ Q♦ J♦ to Q♦ J♦.

16.　6♣ 7♣ 8♦ T♣ J♦. This hand contains two alternative 4-card inside straights, 6♣ 7♣ 8♦ T♣ and 7♣ 8♦ T♣ J♦. Since the first one of these contains no high cards and the second contains one, it is intuitive as well as being explicit in Principle # 9 (c) that the combination with one high card is preferable to the one with no high cards. However, this hand also contains a 3-card straight flush with two gaps and no high cards, 6♣ 7♣ T♣. We know from Principle # 11 (d) that a straight flush like this has more value than an inside straight with no high cards, but less value than an inside straight with one high card. Prefer 7♣ 8♦ T♣ J♦ to 6♣ 7♣ T♣.

17.　A♥ J♥ 5♦ 4♦ 3♦. You may know that, in Jacks or Better, a consecutive 3-card straight flush is more valuable than two suited high cards. This principle is reinforced in Double Bonus where the flush and the straight both pay extra. Holding 5♦ 4♦ 3♦ rather than A♥ J♥ is something that we know we must do, but which we may know from experience seldom leads anywhere. In fact there is an 87% chance of ending up with nothing from 5♦ 4♦ 3♦ compared to only 61% from A♥ J♥. If you think that the main reason for holding this combination is the prospect of getting a straight flush, you are likely to be disappointed. On average, you are going to have to play this type of combination 360 times before connecting on a straight flush. Most of the return from 5♦ 4♦ 3♦ comes from the chances of completing a flush or a straight. If you were playing

Hundred Play, you would expect to get around four of each. You would be unlikely to get your total money back, but you would normally do a lot better than holding A♥ J♥. The probability that A♥ J♥ will produce a royal is less than 1 in 16,000 (or 1 in 1,600 in Hundred Play), which is also the probability that it will produce quad aces.

18. Q♥ K♦ 6♣ 5♣ T♥. If you were dealt this hand in Jacks or Better, you would always prefer Q♥ K♦ to Q♥ T♥. However, in Double Bonus, the extra payout on the flush and the straight adds considerably more value to Q♥ T♥ than to Q♥ K♦. We know from Principle # 10 that the Q♥ T♥ has more value than Q♥ K♦. We also know from this principle that, if we were to change this hand to Q♥ J♦ 6♣ 5♣ T♥, the Q♥ J♦ T♥ would have been preferable to both Q♥ J♦ and Q♥ T♥.

19. T♥ Q♦ 9♥ K♣ 7♥. Hand options that contain face cards and aces always seem to stand out more than options that contain only low cards. In this hand, the 4-card inside straight with two high cards, T♥ Q♦ 9♥ K♣, is plain to see. Less noticeable is the 3-card straight flush, T♥ 9♥ 7♥. Since this only has one gap, Principle # 11 (c) tells us that it is preferable to any combination of unsuited high cards or any 4-card inside straight. Prefer T♥ 9♥ 7♥ to T♥ Q♦ 9♥ K♣.

20. 7♣ K♦ J♣ Q♥ 8♣. It is easy to notice K♦ J♣ Q♥ in this hand. We know from Principle # 7 (a) that when you are dealt KQJ of different suits, hold all three cards. However, like most of the principles, there is an implicit assumption that there is no higher ranking combination in the hand. If you are playing quickly, you may miss the fact that the 3-card straight flush, 7♣ J♣ 8♣, is tucked away in the hand. This 3-card straight flush includes a high card and is covered on line 8 of the Recreational Strategy table, while unsuited KQJ is covered on line 15. Prefer 7♣ J♣ 8♣ to K♦ J♣ Q♥.

3.4. Recreational Strategy Practice Session

It is time to test yourself again to see whether you are ready to proceed to Level 3: "Basic Strategy." As before, the number at the beginning of each line indicates where the correct answer is to be found in the answer column and all answers are correct for 10/7, 9/7, and 10/7/80 games at higher strategy levels.

Question							Answer				
17.	J♦	Q♦	9♣	7♥	K♠	1.	K♣	J♣	T♣		9♣
4.	6♦	8♣	T♦	3♦	7♥	2.				A♣	
20.	J♦	8♣	T♦	9♦	8♥	3.	A♣			A♥	A♦
11.	T♦	A♦	J♦	5♦	Q♦	4.	6♦	8♣	T♦		7♥
16.	J♣	2♥	A♥	3♠	T♣	5.		7♦		8♦	4♦
3.	A♣	5♣	5♦	A♥	A♦	6.	6♦		A♦		T♦
19.	J♦	Q♦	T♥	6♥	8♥	7.	T♣	9♣	K♠		Q♥
10.	9♥	9♦	T♠	J♠	Q♠	8.	K♣		Q♣		
1.	K♠	J♣	T♣	J♥	9♣	9.	Q♣		A♣		8♣
12.	A♥	4♥	K♣	3♠	5♦	10.		T♠	J♠	Q♠	
6.	6♦	8♣	A♦	7♣	T♦	11.	T♦	A♦	J♦		Q♦
18.	A♥	Q♣	5♥	J♠	7♥	12.	A♥	4♥		3♠	5♦
15.	3♣	5♣	4♣	A♦	A♣	13.		T♠	K♣	Q♣	A♦
2.	3♥	4♥	6♠	A♣	7♣	14.	T♥	J♥		9♥	5♥
8.	K♣	7♠	J♦	Q♣	8♦	15.	3♣	5♣	4♣		A♣
5.	Q♠	7♦	K♣	8♦	4♦	16.	J♣				T♣
13.	2♣	T♠	K♣	Q♣	A♦	17.	J♦	Q♦	9♣		K♠
7.	T♣	9♣	K♠	8♠	Q♥	18.		Q♣		J♠	
14.	T♥	J♥	8♣	9♥	5♥	19.	J♦	Q♦			
9.	Q♣	T♦	A♣	9♦	8♣	20.	J♦ 8♣ T♦ 9♦ or J♦ T♦ 9♦ 8♥				

Chapter 4

Level 3: Introduction to "Basic Strategy"

This chapter follows very closely chapter 4 of the Jacks or Better Winner's Guide. All these Guides, together with the Dancer/Daily Strategy Cards, use common notation. There are only two main differences in the notation used in Double Bonus to that used in Jacks or Better. First, 3-card flushes (FL3) are held in Double Bonus and are distinguished by whether they contain zero, one, or two high cards (FL3 0hi, FL3 1hi, or FL3 2hi respectively). Second, 4-card inside straights with zero, one, or two high cards are held in Double Bonus and are represented by ST4i 0hi, ST4i 1hi, and ST4i 2hi respectively. If you are familiar with our notation and also understand what is meant by "Basic Strategy," you may wish to skip to chapter 5.

4.1. The Meaning of "Basic Strategy"

If you were able to watch a computer playing 10/7 perfectly, you might occasionally notice some strange things. For example, from K♣ J♣ 8♥ 6♣ 5♥, it would hold K♣ J♣, while from K♣ J♣ 9♥ 6♣ 5♥, it would hold K♣ J♣ 6♣. Why should it switch from holding K♣ J♣ in the first case to K♣ J♣ 6♣ in the second? The only card in the hand that is changed is the 8♥, which has become the 9♥. The 8♥ has no influence on any paying combination that K♣ J♣ has the possibility of becoming. However, when we change it to the 9♥, the potential for K♣ J♣ to become a KQJT9 straight is reduced because the remaining pack now only has three 9s rather than four. Although the presence of the 9♥ reduces the value of K♣ J♣, it has no effect on the value of K♣ J♣ 6♣. The 9♥ is an example of a "penalty card" – it penalizes the potential of K♣ J♣ to become a KQJT9 straight and makes K♣ J♣ 6♣ preferable to K♣ J♣. Penalty cards are discussed more fully in Level 4: "Advanced Strategy."

The Basic Strategy is the highest level of strategy that is possible without penalty cards situations being included in the strategy. This does not mean that penalty cards have not been considered in devising the strategy. On the contrary, the Basic Strategy has taken account of all situations in which penalty cards affect the appropriate choice of hand. These flip-flop situations have all been calculated according to their likelihood and their values, and presumptions have then been calculated regarding the rankings of the overall hand types.

The Basic Strategy will not always give you the correct answer, but it will tell you the combination that is preferable if you wish always to play the hand type the same way. In the Basic Strategy table, the combination K♣ J♣ 6♣ is included in the category FL3 2hi, which is found on line 11. K♣ J♣ is covered on line 12. In other words, K♣ J♣ 6♣ is ranked higher than K♣ J♣. This means that you will be better off if you always prefer K♣ J♣ 6♣ to K♣ J♣ rather than the other way around. Sometimes, you will be incorrect, but you will get a higher return in the long term if you always do it this way rather than the opposite way.

There are many experienced players who choose to play at the Basic Strategy level rather than the Advanced — they prefer to ignore penalty cards. In Double Bonus, the theoretical return from Basic Strategy play is only around two hundredths of a percent below computer-perfect Advanced Strategy.

4.2. Notation

4.2.1. Hand type notation

The Level 3 and 4 strategies contain a lot of information. In order to reduce the amount of space they take up, hand types are abbreviated from words to symbols. Many other notational conventions are also included. These conventions were originally introduced in the Dancer/Daily Strategy Cards, which first appeared in the year 2000. Once readers are familiar with their meanings, we believe these conventions help the learning process and simplify the strategy tables. Here are the abbreviations that are used for different hand types:

RF = royal flush; SF = straight flush; FL = flush; ST = straight

Whenever one of the above symbols appears, it is always followed immediately by a number representing the number of cards. For example, a complete royal flush with all five cards is represented by RF5; a 4-card royal flush is presented by RF4; and a 3-card royal is presented by RF3. Although it is sometimes convenient in the text to talk about 2-card royal flushes as the group of hand types including such combinations as K♣ Q♣ and J♠ T♠, the symbol RF2 is not used in the strategy tables.

Similarly, SF5 represents a complete 5-card straight flush, while SF4 and SF3 represent 4-card and 3-card straight flushes respectively. A complete 5-card flush or 5-card straight is represented by FL5 or ST5 respectively, while a 4-card flush or straight is represented by FL4 or ST4.

You will notice that 4-of-a-kind, full house, 3-of-a-kind, two pair and high pair are not abbreviated. The reason for this is that they never appear in the strategy except in their complete paying form. It is never necessary to describe a hand type as being an incomplete one of these paying combinations. Whereas it is meaningful to think in terms of a FL4 as being one step away from being a paying FL5, it is not meaningful to define a combination as, say, an incomplete full house.

On occasions, the symbol "H" is used to indicate a high card. When it is used after a specific high card has been designated, it refers to the alternative high cards of lower rank that can accompany the designated high card. For example, two unsuited high cards of which one is an ace could be presented as AK, AQ, or AJ. The term AH covers all these three possibilities. Similarly, KH represents KQ or KJ. Note the KH does not include KA because the A is not lower in rank than the K. Also, it does not include KT because the T is not a high card. A good example of the benefit of using this abbreviation is found when we wish to speak of a 4-card inside straight that contains three high cards of which one is an A. Although we could use "AKQT, AKJT, AQJT," it is more convenient simply to use AHHT. When not preceded by a specific high card, "H" refers to any high card.

4.2.2. Suited versus unsuited cards

It is important to distinguish combinations of cards that are all-of-the-same-suit ("suited") or not-all-of-the-same-suit ("unsuited"). As in the Dancer/Daily Strategy Cards, we adopt the convention of using **bold italics** to indicate suited, while using a "normal" typeface to indicate unsuited. For example, Q♦ J♦ can be represented by **QJ**, while Q♥ J♠ can be represented by QJ. Also **HH** represents any two suited high cards, while HH represents any two unsuited high cards.

When we say that "unsuited" refers to cards that are not-all-of-the-same-suit, this does not necessarily mean that the cards are all of different suits. For example, the combination 3♣ 4♦ 5♣ 6♣ is a ST4 in which not all of the cards are of the same suit. It could be represented simply by 3456. Once the combination contains more than one suit, it doesn't matter how many suits there are – there is no longer any chance of obtaining a flush or straight flush. The combination 3♣ 4♦ 5♣ 6♣ also contains the SF3, 3♣ 5♣ 6♣, which could be represented simply by **356**. The fact that **356** is referring in this case to a SF3 in clubs rather than any other suit has no bearing on strategy.

There are occasions when it is necessary to distinguish two sets of suited cards in the same hand. For example, in the hand 3♥ 4♥ 5♥ A♦ K♦, there is the consideration of whether **345** is preferable to **AK**. When bold italics have already been used in the hand, confusion is avoided by distinguishing suited cards by the use of quotes. This hand may be identified as "345" **AK**, or, equivalently, **AK** "345".

It is sometimes necessary to distinguish a card of the same suit that cannot form part of a straight flush with the preceding cards in the combination. This is represented by **x**. For example, **QTx** is a 3-card flush that includes **QT** plus one other card, such as Q♥ T♥ 5♥. Note that if this third card had been a 9♥ or an 8♥, as in Q♥ T♥ 8♥, it would NOT have been appropriate to denote this as **QTx**. Instead, it would be represented as some form of SF3.

The symbol "**x**" is used frequently when comparing 3-card royal flushes to 4-card flushes. For example, when **KQJ** is extended into a 4-card flush, this flush can be represented by **KQJx**.

4.2.3. Insides

We have already started using the word "inside" in relation to 4-card straights. We now need to extend this discussion. Consider the combinations 2♣ 3♣ 4♣ and 2♦ 3♦ 5♦. Both of these are types of SF3. The first is consecutive, while the second has a gap. However, they both have exactly the same value since they have identical opportunities to become paying straights and straight flushes (as well as flushes, high pairs, two pairs, and 3-of-a-kinds). For each, there are two straights or straight flushes that they could become, and they are A2345 and 23456.

Normally, a SF3 with no gap has the possibility of becoming three different straights or straight flushes. For example, 6♥ 7♥ 8♥ may become 45678, 56789, or 6789T. However, 2♣ 3♣ 4♣ has the problem that it bumps up against the A at the low end. Because it only has the potential to become two rather than three straights or straight flushes, it is "as if" it contained a gap, just like 2♦ 3♦ 5♦.

The term "inside" is used in preference to "gap" to allow combinations like 2♣ 3♣ 4♣ and 2♦ 3♦ 5♦ to be grouped together as combinations of equal value possessing "a single inside."

The term "open-ended" was introduced earlier as referring to a 4-card straight that can be completed from above or below. "Open-ended" and "non-inside" are synonymous. There are two 3-card straights that are held in Double Bonus and they are KQJ and QJT. These are always identified specifically as KQJ and QJT rather than as ST3s. We only use the terms "open-ended straights" and "inside straights" when we are talking about 4-card straights. However, when talking about 3-card straight flushes, the term open-ended would need to be confined to combinations that could be extended both two ranks higher and two ranks lower. Although the hand option 2♣ 3♣ 4♣ looks open ended at first glance, it can only be extended one rank lower. When talking about a 3-card straight flush, we use the terms "non-inside," "single inside," and "double inside."

Any ST4 that contains an ace has the possibility of being completed only with a single ranked card and therefore must be considered to contain an inside. A♣ 2♦ 3♥ 4♠ and A♥ 2♣ 4♦ 5♥ are both 4-card inside straights with one high card and are included in the category "ST4i 1hi." Also in this category would be included combinations such as J♥ T♥ 8♣ 7♠ and Q♣ T♠ 9♦ 8♥.

A 4-card inside straight with two high cards is represented by ST4i 2hi and includes combinations such as K♠ Q♦ T♦ 9♥ and Q♥ J♣ T♥ 8♦.

When a 4-card inside straight includes three high cards, it must be of the form AHHT or KQJ9. These two forms are used instead of ST4i 3hi. Similarly, when containing four high cards, it could be represented by ST4i 4hi. However, since this must take the form of AKQJ, it is clearer to present it as such.

Any SF3 with A-low must be considered to be double inside. For example, A♣ 2♣ 3♣ and A♦ 3♦ 5♦ have identical values and each contain two insides. It might seem that *A35* has more insides than does *A23*, but the only straight or straight flush either one may be part of is A2345. It is easy to see that 2 and 4 are the two insides in *A35*, but not so easy to see that 4 and 5 make up the two insides in *A23*.

4.2.4. The problem with SF3s

SF3s may have zero, one, or two insides, and zero, one, or two high cards. There are actually eight different combinations of insides and high cards. In order to simplify the appearance of SF3s within strategies, the Dancer/Daily Strategy Cards introduced a convention to simplify this unwieldy situation.

Each inside decreases the value of a SF3 combination. In the absence of high cards, a 3-card straight flush with two insides is worth less than one with one inside, which in turn is worth less than one with no insides. In contrast, every high card adds value to the combination. The negative value brought on by an extra inside is fairly close to the positive value brought on by an extra high card. In a sense, one extra high card can be traded off for one extra inside. For this reason, we distinguish SF3s by the number of high cards minus the number of insides. This number is placed after SF3 and may be +1, +0, -1, or -2.

Every SF3 designation is followed by a number equal to the number of high cards minus the number of insides.

SF3 +1.   This is a SF3 that has a number of high cards that is one greater than the number of insides. It might be two high cards and one inside or one high card with no insides. The only possible SF3 +1 combinations are *QJ9* and *JT9*.

SF3 +0.   This is a combination with an equal number of high cards and insides. It might be two of each, such as *KQ9* or *QJ8*, one of each, such as *QT9* or *J98*, or none of each such as *345* or *89T*. You may wonder why we do not omit the zero altogether after the SF3, or simply put "0" rather than "+0". The reason for including the zero is that SF3 by itself is a generic abbreviation for a 3-card straight flush without any requirement of insides or high cards. We include the "+" so that the different SF3s have the same general appearance. As long as we are going to add a sign, we prefer the look of "SF3 +0" to "SF3 -0" even though they have the same value.

SF3 -1.   This is a combination with one fewer high card than insides. It might be one high card and two insides, such as *QT8* or *J87*, or no high cards and one inside, such as *457* or *79T*. It is important to note that all A-low combinations such as *A23* or *A45* contain two insides and have one high card, and therefore fit into this category.

SF3 -2.   This is always a combination with no high cards and two insides, such as *246* or *69T*.

This shorthand allows us to reduce the normal eight entries for 3-card straight flushes to four entries. Memorizing four locations on a strategy table is much easier than memorizing eight. The old format for representing SF3s was to include both the number of insides and the number of high cards. In this old system, it was easy to confuse on a strategy table, for example, SF3 1i 2hi with SF3 2i 1 hi. In the new system, the first translates to SF3 +1, which is easily distinguishable and quite a bit more valuable than the second one, which translates to SF3 -1.

4.2.5. The meaning of ">" and "<"

A large number of combinations are identified in the Level 3 and 4 strategies. To reduce the number of lines of strategy, more than one combination may appear on a single line. Often, these combinations are mutually exclusive. Line 1 of the Basic Strategy identifies three hand types that are separated by semicolons:

RF5; SF5; 4-OF-A-KIND;

If you are dealt a RF5, you cannot also have a SF5 or a 4-of-a-kind. Although RF5 is worth more than the other two, it is not necessary for strategy purposes to make this distinction. The line of strategy above tells you simply to hold any one of these hands if dealt. There is no conflict between these hands.

In contrast, line 2 is as follows:

RF4 > FL5 and ST5 > SF4 any

The symbol ">" (which mathematicians recognize as meaning "greater than") means that whatever is on the left side of the symbol has greater expected value than whatever is on the right. In Level 4, the symbol "<" is used on many occasions and means the opposite, with whatever is on the left having lower expected value than whatever is on the right.

In the hand A♣ Q♣ J♣ T♣ 8♣, a RF4 and a FL5 are both present. In line 2 of the Basic Strategy table, the symbol ">" is used to show that the RF4, A♣ Q♣ J♣ T♣, has greater value than the FL5, A♣ Q♣ J♣ T♣ 8♣. Similarly, a RF4 has greater value than a ST5.

Although FL5 and ST5 cannot coexist in the same hand, each of them may be accompanied by a SF4. The depiction, "FL5 and ST5 > SF4 any," means that you do not need to worry about whether FL5 is superior or inferior to ST5, but you do need to be aware that they are both superior to any SF4.

There are many different words that we use in the text as synonymous with "of greater expected value." They do not have any purpose other than to avoid incessant repetition. These include words such as 'preferable', 'superior', 'better', 'more valuable', etc.

Chapter 5

Level 3: "Basic Strategy" for 10/7 and 9/7 Double Bonus

5.1. Basic Strategy Table for 10/7 and 9/7

Select the hand option that appears highest in the following list:

1:	RF5; SF5; 4-OF-A-KIND
2:	RF4 > FL5 and ST5 > SF4 any
3:	AAA > FULL HOUSE > 3-OF-A-KIND others
4:	TWO PAIR > AA in 10/7, but TWO PAIR < AA in 9/7
5a*:	*QJT* > FL4 all > RF3 others
5b*:	*KQJ*, *QJT* > KK, QQ, JJ > RF3 others
5c*:	FL4 3hi (also 2hi in 9/7) > KK, QQ, JJ > FL4 others
6:	ST4 non-inside [2345 – KQJT]
7:	low pair [22 – 44] > SF3 +1 [*JT9*, *QJ9*] > low pair [55 – TT]
8:	AKQJ > SF3+0
9:	AHHT, KQJ9
10:	*QJ*
11:	FL3 2hi
12:	*KH*
13:	SF3 -1 [includes *234* and all A-low]
14:	*AH*
15:	KQJ; ST4i 2hi > ST4i 1hi
16:	QJT > QJ, *JT*, *QT* (*QT* always < *QTx*)
17:	SF3 -2
18:	FL3 1hi
19:	KH
20:	A
21:	*KT*
22:	K, Q, J
23:	ST4i 0hi > FL3 0hi
24:	five new cards

*   Lines 5a, 5b, and 5c cover those situations in which a hand contains any two of the three combinations: {KK, QQ, JJ}, FL4, and RF3. If all three are present, use the following rule:

> "If the RF3 is *QJT*, hold *QJT*. If the RF3 is other than *QJT*, the preferred combination is either {KK, QQ, JJ} or FL4, and can be determined from line 5c alone."

5.2. The Relationships between High Pairs, RF3, and FL4

Principle # 3 tells us that high pairs, 3-card royal flushes, and 4-card flushes are preferable to all non-paying combinations except for 4-card royal flushes and 4-card straight flushes. This is the same as in Jacks or Better. However, where Double Bonus and Jacks or Better differ is in the relationship between these three combinations. In Jacks or Better, high pairs are always more valuable than 3-card royals, which are almost always more valuable than 4-card flushes. In Double Bonus, the Beginner and Recreational Strategy tables place a 4-card flush above a 3-card royal, although this was pointed out to be a stopgap measure until the full relationship was explored in this level.

There is no change or exception to the supremacy of a pair of aces. Principle # 2 instructs us to break a pair of aces only for a 4-card royal flush or a 4-card straight flush. As such, a pair of aces is always preferable to a 4-card flush or a 3-card royal flush. In this section, we will be looking at the high pairs, {KK, QQ, JJ}.

In Double Bonus, the value of high pairs, {KK, QQ, JJ}, is lower than in Jacks or Better owing to the reduced payout on two pair. The negative impact of two pair is far greater than the positive impact that comes from the higher payouts on quads and, in the case of 10/7, full houses. In contrast, the values of both 4-card flushes and 3-card royal flushes are both increased in Double Bonus compared with Jacks or Better. The higher payout on the flush is felt most strongly in the value of 4-card flushes. The value of 3-card royal flush is raised by a much smaller amount, but is also raised by the higher payout on the straight. The result of these factors is that the previously third place 4-card flush and second place 3-card royal are raised in value such that they are neck and neck both with each other and with {KK, QQ, JJ}.

The decrease in the value of {KK, QQ, JJ} is greater in 9/7 than in 10/7. Depending upon the nature of the 3-card royal and the 4-card flush, and whether the game is 10/7 or 9/7, any one of these three hand options may be the preferred play. There is also the consideration that all three may be present in the same hand. This all gives rise to a confusing situation. For readers who intend moving on from the Basic Strategy to the Advanced Strategy, the good news is that, once you learn the rules presented here, you have them down perfectly. There will be no need to update your knowledge in this particular area when you progress to Level 4 (except for some oddball exceptions when the straight flush pays 80 rather than 50). Before we begin the discussion, it is instructive to consider why it is that 3-card royals and 4-card flushes have different values depending upon their precise form.

In the previous chapter, we saw how the value of a 3-card straight flush depends upon both its number of high cards and its number of insides. We also noted that a 3-card straight flush with A-low must be considered to be double inside. Similar arguments apply to 3-card royal flushes.

Any RF3 that includes as ace must be considered to have two insides. For example, when it is of the form **AQT**, it is easy to see that the two insides are K and J. Both a K and a J are necessary to complete a straight, and if they are both of the appropriate suit, they will complete the royal. There is one and only one straight that **AQT** can become and that is AKQJT. When the RF3 is, say, **AKQ**, it still only has the potential to form one straight, AKQJT. Although the J and T that are needed to complete the straight seem to be on the outside, they nevertheless represent two insides.

All A-high RF3 fit into one of two categories. First, there is **AHT**, which includes **AKT**, **AQT**, and **AJT**; second, there is **AHH**, which includes **AKQ**, **AKJ**, and **AQJ**. These two forms both have two insides, but **AHH** has three high cards and has a higher expected value than **AHT**, which only has two high cards. From a strategy point of view, all **AHH** have a single relationship with high pairs and 4-card flushes, as do all **AHT**.

When a RF3 is K-high, it must be considered to be single inside. There are only three RF3s that can be K-high and they are **KQJ**, **KQT**, and **KJT**. All three have the same potential to form two straights, AKQJT and KQJT9. Although **KQJ** could be covered by **KHH**, there is no other RF3 in this category and so using **KHH** would bring no gain in efficiency. **KQT** and **KJT** are together covered by **KHT**. Because **KQJ** has three high cards and one inside, while **KHT** has only two high cards and one inside, **KQJ** has a higher expected value than **KHT**.

When a RF3 is Q-high, it must be **QJT** and has two high cards and no insides.

It is interesting to note that, just as in the case of 3-card straight flushes, the values of these various 3-card royal combinations depend upon the number of high cards minus the number of insides. In the absence of any interference from other cards in the hand, they have the following $EVs in 10/7 Double Bonus:

two more high cards than insides:	**QJT** = $7.92;	**KQJ** = $7.88
one more high card than insides:	**KHT** = $7.38;	**AHH** = $7.33
equal number of high cards and insides:	**AHT** = $6.83	

When in competition with a high pair, it is not surprising that **QJT** and **KQJ** are on the same rung of the ladder. In the absence of a FL4 also being present, we will see that they are both always preferable to {KK, QQ, JJ}, while **KHT** and **AHH** (as well as **AHT**) are always less preferable.

Unfortunately, it is not as easy as simply categorizing RF3s in terms of a number equal to the difference between the number of high cards and the number of insides. The reason for this is that each type of RF3 can be part of a FL4. For example, **QJT** can be part of **QJTx**, while **KQJ** can be part of **KQJx**. These two 4-card flushes differ in value because **QJTx** has two high cards, and is of less lower value than **KQJx**, which has three high cards. We will see that, although both **QJT** and **KQJ** are preferable to {KK, QQ, JJ}, **QJT** is more valuable than **QJTx**, while **KQJ** is less valuable than **KQJx**.

We appreciate that the above discussion may have been confusing. In the following sections, we are going to explain "what" the relationships are between {KK, QQ, JJ}, RF3s, and FL4s with the above discussion covering "why" they are what they are. We will begin the discussion by looking at the relationships when only two of the three combinations are present in the same hand. We will then look at the relationships when all three are present.

Since these relationships are very important in Double Bonus and remain unchanged in the Advanced Strategy (with only slight exceptions in 10/7/80), we are going to add them to the General Principles, beginning at # 13.

5.2.1. Relationship between {KK, QQ, JJ}, RF3, and FL4 when only two are present.

Principle # 13

> **When no high pair is present, prefer 4-card flushes to all 3-card royal flushes other than *QJT*.**

From line 5a of the Basic Strategy table, we have the somewhat surprising result that *QJT* is the only 3-card royal flush that is ever preferable to a 4-card flush of which it can be a part. The reason for this is that *QJT* is the most valuable 3-card royal flush, while the 4-card flush of which it can be part of is one of the lesser-valued ones that has two rather than three high cards. For example:

from Q♣ J♣ T♣ 7♣ 3♥	prefer Q♣ J♣ T♣ to Q♣ J♣ T♣ 7♣
from A♠ J♠ T♠ 9♠ 5♣	extend A♠ J♠ T♠ into A♠ J♠ T♠ 9♠
from K♦ Q♦ J♦ T♥ 7♦	extend K♦ Q♦ J♦ into K♦ Q♦ J♦ 7♦
from A♥ Q♥ J♥ 2♥ 2♠	extend A♥ Q♥ J♥ into A♥ Q♥ J♥ 2♥
from Q♦ J♦ T♦ 5♣ 8♦	be sure to hold the SF4, Q♦ J♦ T♦ 8♦

In the first two examples above, the hands contain a 4-card flush that contains a 3-card royal flush and a 3-card straight flush. Any 4-card flush is worth more than the strongest SF3, such as J♠ T♠ 9♠. In the third example, the hand also contains the strongest of all 4-card open-ended straights, K♦ Q♦ J♦ T♥. Again any FL4 or RF3 is worth more than any ST4. In the fourth example, the hand contains a low pair, which again has less value than any FL4 or RF3. In the last example, it is appropriate to add the fourth flush card to *QJT* because it forms part of a 4-card straight flush.

Principle # 14

> **When no 4-card flush is present, prefer {KK, QQ, JJ} to all 3-card royal flushes except *QJT* and *KQJ*.**

We pointed out in the previous section that **KQJ** and **QJT** are the most valuable 3-card royals. With the flush paying 7 rather than 6 in Double Bonus, this alone raises their values above that of {KK, QQ, JJ}. This is reinforced by the straight paying 5 rather than 4. This relationship is given in line 5b of the Basic Strategy table. For example:

from K♣ Q♣ J♣ T♦ J♥	prefer K♣ Q♣ J♣ to J♣ J♥
from Q♦ Q♥ J♥ T♥ 9♣	prefer Q♥ J♥ T♥ to Q♦ Q♥
from A♦ K♦ Q♦ Q♣ 5♥	prefer Q♦ Q♣ to A♦ K♦ Q♦
from K♠ Q♠ T♠ J♣ Q♦	prefer Q♠ Q♦ to K♠ Q♠ T♠
from K♥ Q♥ J♥ J♣ 9♥	be sure to hold the SF4, K♥ Q♥ J♥ 9♥
from K♦ J♦ T♦ K♠ T♣	be sure to hold the two pair, K♦ T♦ K♠ T♣
from Q♥ J♥ T♥ A♣ A♦	always prefer a pair of aces to any RF3 or FL4

Principle # 15

When no 3-card royal flush is present, prefer {KK, QQ, JJ} to a 4-card flush unless the 4-card flush contains three high cards (also two high cards in 9/7)

We see here that there is a difference between 10/7 and 9/7. High pairs are worth more in 10/7 than in 9/7 because of the possibility that they may turn into full houses with the higher payout. Whereas a FL4 needs to have three high cards in 10/7 to be of greater value than {KK, QQ, JJ}, two high cards are sufficient in 9/7.

Principle # 15 also applies to situations in which a RF3 is not present and the FL4 contains one or two high cards. For example, from K♣ K♦ Q♣ 7♣ 3♣, hold K♣ K♦ in 10/7, but hold K♣ Q♣ 7♣ 3♣ in 9/7. From J♥ J♠ 9♥ 7♥ 3♥, prefer J♥ J♠ to J♥ 9♥ 7♥ 3♥ in both 10/7 and 9/7. These relationships are given in line 5c of the Basic Strategy table.

5.2.2. Relationship between {KK, QQ, JJ}, RF3, and FL4 when all three are present.

On the original version of the Dancer/Daily Double Bonus Strategy Card, we included the following footnote to lines 5a, b, and c:

"When a hand contains the three alternatives, RF3, FL4, and {KK, QQ, JJ}, use any of these three rules to eliminate one alternative. The remaining two alternatives will then be covered by a single rule."

For example, in the hand K♣ Q♣ J♣ 5♣ J♥, the alternatives are: the RF3, K♣ Q♣ J♣; the FL4, K♣ Q♣ J♣ 5♣; and the J♣ J♥. If we take line 5a first, we know that 4-card flushes are preferable to all three card royals other than **QJT**. This means that K♣ Q♣ J♣ 5♣ is preferable to K♣ Q♣ J♣. This leaves us with just K♣ Q♣ J♣ 5♣ and

57

J♣ J♥. The relationship between FL4 and {KK, QQ, JJ} is covered on line 5c. Because K♣ Q♣ J♣ 5♣ has three high cards, it is preferable to J♣ J♥ in both 10/7 and 9/7.

We could have approached this hand by beginning with any one of the three rules comprising line 5. If we had begun with, say, line 5b instead of 5a, we would have eliminated J♣ J♥ as being inferior to K♣ Q♣ J♣, and we would have been left with K♣ Q♣ J♣ 5♣ and K♣ Q♣ J♣, which is covered on line 5a. Again we would have determined that the preferred combination is K♣ Q♣ J♣ 5♣.

For Liam W. Daily, this approach works well. He knows the three rules by heart. When he is faced with all three combinations in the same hand, he compares any two of the three, determines which of the two has more value, and then compares it to the remaining one.

For Bob Dancer, however, this is unnecessarily complicated. Even though he also has the three rules memorized, he finds it easier to remember that *QJT* provides the only exception to the rule contained in line 5c than it is to apply two of the rules separately. Although this original footnote remains 100% accurate, we have changed the footnote in this Winner's Guide to the following:

"Lines 5a, 5b, and 5c cover those situations in which a hand contains any two of the three combinations: {KK, QQ, JJ}, FL4, and RF3. If all three are present, use the following rule:

If the RF3 is *QJT*, hold *QJT*. If the RF3 is other than *QJT*, the preferred combination is either {KK, QQ, JJ} or FL4, and can be determined from line 5c alone."

This rule will always give the same correct answer as the original footnote and we think that most players will prefer this presentation.

When faced with all three combinations in the same hand, the first thing to do is to look to see whether it contains *QJT*. If it does, your task is complete. Always prefer *QJT* to both {KK, QQ, JJ} and FL4 (which in this case would be of the form *QJTx*).

If the RF3 is anything other than *QJT*, the RF3 is NOT going to be the preferred combination. The most valuable of the three combinations in the hand will be either {KK, QQ, JJ} or FL4, not the RF3. The determination of the preferred combination is a simple application of line 5c. In other words,

"If no *QJT*, just use 5c."

After applying line 5c, the actual result is a very simple rule for 9/7 where Principle # 15 says that a FL4 only needs a minimum of two high cards to be superior to {KK, QQ, JJ}. Because all 3-card royals contain at least two high cards, all 4-card flushes of which they are a part must contain at least two high cards and be preferable to {KK, QQ, JJ}. We therefore have the rule:

In 9/7 only: When {KK, QQ, JJ}, RF3, and FL4 are together in the same hand, always hold the FL4, except prefer *QJT* to *QJTx*.

Although it is possible to generate a single integrated rule for 10/7, it would be much more complicated than the one above for 9/7. Provided you know line 5c, it is easier to remember, "If no *QJT*, just use 5c."

At first glance, this general preference for 4-card flushes seems to be an about-face from the stopgap instruction in the Beginner and Recreational Strategies to prefer a high pair to FL4. The reason for this apparent change is NOT that we want to keep the lower level strategies as close to Jacks or Better as possible. The reason is that the above rule applies only when a RF3 is also present in the hand. When a high pair is in competition with a FL4 with only one high card, as in K♣ K♦ T♦ 6♦ 3♦, it is a major mistake to hold the flush. Also, when it is a pair of aces, it is a major mistake to prefer a FL4 however many high cards the FL4 may contain (short of there being four cards to a royal).

5.3. Summary of General Principles

There now follows a summary of the General Principles. In a sense, this represents a summary of all the strategy analysis that has gone before. Whereas it is difficult to learn the Basic Strategy table in rote fashion, these principles may be read, considered, and learned one at a time. If you have not played Double Bonus for some time and need a refresher, study this summary. After this, practice on the computer with *Bob Dancer Presents WinPoker*. Before walking into a casino, review these principles, but be sure to take a copy of a strategy table with you (such as the Dancer/Daily Double Bonus Strategy Card) to use as a reference source when you are uncertain of how to play a particular hand. These General Principles apply to 10/7, 9/7, and 10/7/80.

1. Hold all paying combinations of TWO PAIR or higher, except:

    (a) Break a full house only for AAA.

    (b) Break a FLUSH or a STRAIGHT only for a 4-card-royal flush.

    (c) Break TWO PAIR for a pair of aces in 9/7 only. At all other times, prefer TWO PAIR to one pair.

2. Break a pair of aces only for a 4-card royal flush or a 4-card straight flush.

3. The three combinations of {KK, QQ, JJ}, 4-card flush, and 3-card royal flush are preferable to all non-paying combinations except for a 4-card royal flush and a 4-card straight flush.

4. Prefer a consecutive 4-card straight (except A234) to a low pair. Prefer both to two suited high cards or any combination of high cards of mixed suits.

5. Any 3-card straight flush should be extended into a 4-card flush or consecutive 4-card straight (except A234) when possible. Also, prefer a low pair to any 3-card straight flush.

6. Prefer two suited high cards to three high cards of mixed suits.

7. (a) When dealt three high cards of different suits of which one is an ace, discard the ace. When dealt KQJ of different suits, hold all three.

    (b) Prefer two unsuited high cards to one, except, when one of the high cards is an ace, hold only the ace.

    (c) When there is a single high card accompanied by a suited T, hold both the high card and the suited T when the high card is a K, Q or J. Discard the T when the high card is an ace.

8. (a) Extend two suited high cards other than *QJ* into 3-card flushes when possible.

    (b) Always prefer a 3-card flush including *QT* suited to the *QT* by itself. Prefer all other 3-card flushes with one high card to two unsuited high cards or a single high card with suited T, with the exception of the trio of combinations: QJ unsuited, *JT* suited, and *QT* suited.

60

9.   (a)   Always prefer a 4-card open-ended straight to a 4-card inside straight.

      (b)   When a 4-card inside straight has two or three high cards, prefer the inside straight to the high cards except when all the high cards in the inside straight are of the same suit.

      (c)   When two 4-card inside straights occur in the same hand, prefer the one with the extra high card, if any.

10.   (a)   Prefer QJT to: QJ unsuited, *QT* suited, *JT* suited, or any 3-card flush with one high card. However, prefer QJT8 to QJT.

      (b)   Prefer suited *QT* and *JT* to unsuited KQ or KJ, and also to an ace alone.

11.   (a)   Always extend a 2-card royal flush or single high card into a 3-card or 4-card straight flush when possible.

      (b)   Prefer a consecutive 3-card straight flush (except *A23* and *234*) to two suited high cards, to any combination of unsuited high cards, or to any inside straight.

      (c)   Prefer a 3-card straight flush with one gap to any combination of unsuited high cards or any inside straight.

      (d)   A 3-card straight flush with two gaps and no high cards is more valuable than a 4-card inside straight with no high cards, but less valuable than an inside straight with one or two high cards.

      (e)   Prefer a 3-card straight flush with two gaps and no high cards to a single high card, a single high card with suited T, or two unsuited high cards except for the three combinations: QJ unsuited, *QT* suited, and *JT* suited.

12.   (a)   Extend a single high card or high card with suited T into a 4-card inside straight or a 3-card flush when possible; prefer the inside straight to the 3-card flush.

      (b)   Hold a 4-card inside straight with no high cards, or a 3-card flush with no high cards, only if there is absolutely nothing else worth holding in the hand. When both are present in the same hand, prefer the inside straight to the 3-card flush.

13.   When no high pair is present, prefer a 4-card flush to all 3-card royal flushes other than *QJT*.

14.   When no 4-card flush is present, prefer {KK, QQ, JJ} to all 3-card royals flushes except *QJT* and *KQJ*.

15.   When no 3-card royal flush is present, prefer {KK, QQ, JJ} to a 4-card flush unless the 4-card flush contains three high cards (also two high cards in 9/7).

5.4. Exceptions, Extensions, and Additions to the General Principles

The General Principles in the above table apply to 10/7, 9/7, and 10/7/80. The following exceptions, extensions, and additions do not necessarily apply to 10/7/80.

(1)   Prefer a SF3 +1 [*JT9, QJ9*] to a low pair [55 – TT].

In Double Bonus, 3-card straight flushes have more value than they do in Jacks or Better owing to the higher payouts on flushes and straights. In contrast to this, low pairs have less value. While it is true that low pairs may become higher paying quads, this positive benefit is more than offset by the even money payout on two pair.

In the Recreational Strategy table, we placed all low pairs above any 3-card straight flush. However, from line 7 of the Basic Strategy table, we see that:

$$\text{low pair } [22 - 44] > \text{SF3 +1 } [\textit{JT9, QJ9}] > \text{low pair } [55 - TT]$$

The most valuable of all 3-card straight flushes are *JT9* and *QJ9*, which together comprise the set of SF3 +1. These have more value than low pairs [55 – TT] but less value than low pairs [22 – 44]. This distinction between low pairs arises solely from the fact that, when 22 – 44 turn into quads, they pay 400 for a 5-coin bet, while quads arising from 55 – TT pay only 250.

This rule marks one of the many unique features of Double Bonus strategy and there are no exceptions to it when the straight flush pays 50. We will discover in chapter 7 that, when the payout on the straight flush is raised to 80, *JT9* and *QJ9* are preferable to all low pairs.

(2)   Prefer SF3 +0 to any combination of suited or unsuited high cards, or any 4-card inside straight other than AKQJ.

In Jacks or Better, SF3 +0 is preferable to all 4-card inside straights including AKQJ. Although the value of SF3 +0 is higher in Double Bonus owing to the higher payouts on the flush and the straight, the value of AKQJ is raised by an even larger amount. The likelihood of turning AKQJ into an AKQJT straight is greater than the combined likelihood of turning SF3 +0 into a flush or a straight.

Using our SF3 classification system, Principle # 11 (b) instructs us to prefer SF3 +0 to two suited high cards, or any combination of unsuited high cards, or any 4-card inside straight. The only exception to this is AKQJ. For example, in the hand A♣ K♦ Q♥ J♥ 8♥, prefer A♣ K♦ Q♥ J♥ to Q♥ J♥ 8♥. Note that if we change this hand just slightly to A♣ K♦ Q♥ J♥ 9♥, the Q♥ J♥ 9♥ would have been a SF3 +1 and would have been the preferred combination.

If we combine elements of lines 7, 8, 9, and 10 of the Basic Strategy table together, we have:

$$SF3 +1 > AKQJ > SF3+0 > AHHT, KQJ9 > \textbf{\textit{HH}}$$

There are no exceptions to this ranking of hand types in the Advanced Strategy, although we will find that there are in 10/7/80.

(3) Prefer two suited high cards other than *AH* to SF3 -1.

We have discussed previously how *AH* is the least valuable combination of two suited high cards. In general, SF3 -1 has more value than *AH* but less value than *KH* or *QJ*. In the Advanced Strategy, there is an important exception in which *AH* is preferable to SF3 -1, and also a minor exception in which *KH* is less preferable than SF3 -1. *QJ* is always preferable to SF3 -1.

For example:	from	A♦ Q♦ 5♣ 6♣ 8♣	hold 5♣ 6♣ 8♣
	from	K♥ J♥ 6♠ 7♠ 9♠	hold K♥ J♥
	from	Q♥ J♥ 9♦ 7♦ 6♦	hold Q♥ J♥

(4) Prefer SF3 -1 to any combination of unsuited high cards, or a 4-card inside straight with no more than two high cards.

Principle # 11 (c) deals with a 3-card straight flush with one gap. This principle applies to the whole class of SF3 -1. There is an important exception in the Advanced Strategy when SF3 -1 is less valuable than an inside straight with two high cards.

Every A-low 3-card straight flush must be deemed to have two insides. Together with the single high card, this places it in the category of SF3 -1. Since every 4-card straight with A-low must be considered to have an inside, an important implication of this rule is that:

An A-low SF3 is always preferable to an A-low ST4

Here are some examples that deal with the various SF3 -1:

from K♣ Q♦ J♥ 8♥ 7♥	prefer J♥ 8♥ 7♥	to K♣ Q♦ J♥
from A♣ K♣ J♦ T♦ 7♦	prefer A♣ K♣ J♦ T♦	to J♦ T♦ 7♦
from K♣ Q♦ J♠ 9♦ 8♦	prefer K♣ Q♦ J♠ 9♦	to Q♦ 9♦ 8♦
from Q♥ J♦ T♣ 8♣ 7♣	prefer T♣ 8♣ 7♣	to Q♥ J♦ T♣ 8♣
from J♠ T♠ 8♥ 7♠ 6♦	prefer J♠ T♠ 7♠	to J♠ T♠ 8♥ 7♠ or J♠ T♠
from J♥ T♥ 8♠ 7♠ 5♠	prefer 8♠ 7♠ 5♠	to J♥ T♥ 8♠ 7♠ or J♥ T♥
from A♦ 3♦ 4♦ 5♠ 7♣	prefer A♦ 3♦ 4♦	to A♦ 3♦ 4♦ 5♠

5.5. Basic Strategy Examples for 10/7 and 9/7

These hands are presented at random and the order of the cards is sometimes jumbled in a way that makes it harder to recognize all the alternatives. These examples are an important addition to the preceding discussion. They include many situations that straddle more than one of the principles and exceptions.

1.   4♥ 2♦ 5♥ 6♣ A♥. Whenever you are dealt an ace with a cluster of very low cards, always check to see if there is a 4-card inside straight that includes the ace or a 3-card straight flush including the ace. In this hand, both of these options are present in the form of 4♥ 2♦ 5♥ A♥ and 4♥ 5♥ A♥ respectively. We noted in section (4) above that an A-low 3-card straight flush is always preferable to an A-low 4-card straight. This hand also contains a 4-card inside straight with no high cards, 4♥ 2♦ 5♥ 6♣, but this is the least desirable option in the hand. The actual ranking of the options in this hand is: first, 4♥ 5♥ A♥; second, 4♥ 2♦ 5♥ A♥; third, A♥; and fourth, 4♥ 2♦ 5♥ 6♣.

2.   A♦ K♣ Q♥ 2♦ 5♦. When you see the combination, A♦ K♣ Q♥, it is natural to think "this is a high card problem." The 2♦ and 5♦ may look to be of no relevance. We know that, when there are three high cards of different suits of which one is an ace, discard the ace. K♣ Q♥ has more value than A♦ K♣ Q♥. If you hold K♣ Q♥, and then review the remaining cards, you will see that you are about to discard A♦ 2♦ 5♦. This is a SF3 -1, which appears on line 13 of the strategy table – way above K♣ Q♥, which is covered on line 19. Hold A♦ 2♦ 5♦.

3.   Q♥ A♥ T♥ Q♦ 5♥ (pair jacks or better). This is an example of a hand that contains the three combinations: {KK, QQ, JJ}, RF3, and FL4. When all three are present, the preferred combination is determined from the footnote to the Basic Strategy table. This can be summarized as, "If no *QJT*, use 5c." Since there is no *QJT*, line 5c says that a FL4 needs three high cards to be preferable to {KK, QQ, JJ} in 10/7, but only two in 9/7. Since Q♥ A♥ T♥ 5♥ contains only two high cards, it is the preferred combination in 9/7 only. In 10/7, prefer Q♥ Q♦ to Q♥ A♥ T♥ 5♥.

4.   Q♥ J♥ 9♥ 4♣ 4♥. Most mistakes made by experienced players do not arise because they have remembered the strategy incorrectly. They are simply silly mistakes that arise because the player has taken insufficient time to identify all the hand options. A quick look at this hand may tell you that, although the 3-card straight flush is a SF3 +1, the preferred combination is the higher-valued low pair, 4♣ 4♥. This is a major mistake. Of greater value than both the 4♣ 4♥ and the Q♥ J♥ 9♥ is the 4-card flush, Q♥ J♥ 9♥ 4♥.

5.   A♣ K♦ Q♦ A♦ 5♦ (pair jacks or better). This hand contains the pair of aces, A♣ A♦, as well as the 3-card royal, K♦ Q♦ A♦, and the 4-card flush, K♦ Q♦ A♦ 5♦. In contrast to {KK, QQ, JJ}, pairs of aces are on a higher plane than 3-card royals and 4-card flushes. The only non-paying combinations that are preferable to a pair of aces are 4-card royals and 4-card straight flushes. Hold A♣ A♦.

64

6.   J♥ A♣ K♦ Q♥ 8♥ and J♥ A♣ K♦ Q♥ 9♥. We are looking at two hands in this example. The only difference between them is that the 8♥ in the first is replaced with the 9♥ in the second. We pointed out in section (2) above that there are no exceptions to the following important ranking of hand types in either 10/7 or 9/7:

$$SF3 +1> AKQJ > SF3+0 > AHHT, KQJ9 > \textit{HH}$$

Both these hands contain the inside straight, J♥ A♣ K♦ Q♥. Although two of these high cards are suited, J♥ Q♥, we know from Principle # 9 (b) that a 4-card inside straight with two or more high cards has more value than the high cards alone when all the high cards are not of the same suit. J♥ A♣ K♦ Q♥ is therefore preferable to J♥ Q♥. The competition in these hands is between J♥ A♣ K♦ Q♥ and the 3-card straight flush. In the first case, J♥ Q♥ 8♥ has two high cards and two insides and is therefore a SF3 +0, which ranks below J♥ A♣ K♦ Q♥. In the second case, J♥ Q♥ 9♥ again has two high cards but only one inside and is a SF3 +1, which is superior to J♥ A♣ K♦ Q♥.

7.   5♥ 9♦ T♦ 5♠ J♦. The most valuable of all 3-card straight flushes are *JT9* and *QJ9*. Together they comprise the category of SF3 +1. On line 7 of the strategy table, we see that they have greater value than the lesser-valued low pairs, 55 – TT. Prefer 9♦ T♦ J♦ to 5♥ 5♠.

8.   Q♣ T♣ K♣ K♥ 9♣ (pair jacks or better). This hand contains the high pair, K♣ K♥, the 3-card royal, Q♣ J♣ K♣, and the four clubs, Q♣ T♣ K♣ 9♣. However, be sure to recognize that these four clubs are four cards to a straight flush. Both 4-card straight flushes and 4-card royal flushes are preferable to any high pair and every other non-paying combination in both Double Bonus and Jacks or Better. Hold Q♣ J♣ K♣ 9♣.

9.   9♥ J♠ T♠ 7♥ 6♥. When a hand like this appears and you see the J♠ T♠ accompanied by no other high cards and no other cards of the same suit, it is natural to hold it immediately. However, before pressing **DRAW**, be sure to review what you are doing. In Double Bonus, always be on the lookout for cards that will extend a single high card or a high card with suited T into a 4-card inside straight. In this hand, 9♥ J♠ T♠ 7♥ is more valuable than J♠ T♠, but this is still the wrong answer. The hardest type of hand to recognize in most games of video poker is probably a 3-card straight flush that is separated in the hand by something interesting. This is the case in this hand. It doesn't help knowing that SF3 -1 is preferable to both J♠ T♠ and 9♥ J♠ T♠ 7♥ if you don't recognize 9♥ 7♥ 6♥ in the hand. Hold 9♥ 7♥ 6♥ and remind yourself that, even after comparing two likely-looking options, there may still be a third, or even a fourth.

10.   T♦ J♦ Q♦ Q♣ T♥ (two pair). If you hear the machine "ding" when this hand appears, you are making a big mistake if you think it is informing you that you have the high pair, Q♦ Q♣. Always check to see whether there is a second pair to accompany a high pair. Although this hand contains one of the most valuable 3-card royals, T♦ J♦ Q♦, this has significantly less value than two pair. Except when two pair contains aces and the game is 9/7, always hold two pair. Hold T♦ Q♦ Q♣ T♥.

11.   A♦ K♦ 6♣ 5♣ 3♣. In the Basic Strategy table, SF3 -1 appears above *AH* but below *KH* or *QJ*. In this hand, prefer 6♣ 5♣ 3♣ to A♦ K♦. If this hand were changed to Q♦ K♦ 6♣ 5♣ 3♣, the 6♣ 5♣ 3♣ would have been of less value than Q♦ K♦.

12.   J♦ Q♥ K♣ 7♦ 9♦. It is very easy to spot J♦ Q♥ K♣ is this hand, but surprising to discover that this is the third best alternative in the hand. From Principle # 9 (b), we know that a 4-card inside straight with three high cards is preferable to the high cards alone provided the high cards are not-all-of-the-same-suit. J♦ Q♥ K♣ 9♦ is therefore preferable to J♦ Q♥ K♣. However, there is also another combination in this hand that is easy to miss but which should be considered, and that is the 3-card straight flush, J♦ 7♦ 9♦. With one high card and two insides, this is a SF3 -1. Although SF3 -1 appears above KQJ in the strategy table, it is below KQJ9. The preferred combination in this hand is therefore, J♦ Q♥ K♣ 9♦.

   If this hand were changed to J♦ Q♥ K♣ 7♦ 8♦, there would have been no inside straight. The choice would have been between J♦ Q♥ K♣ and J♦ 7♦ 8♦. A SF3 -1 such as J♦ 7♦ 8♦ is preferable to any combination of unsuited high cards such as J♦ Q♥ K♣.

13.   T♣ Q♥ J♥ 9♥ 9♠. When examining this hand, it is easy to focus your attention on what kind of SF3 is Q♥ J♥ 9♥ and whether it has more of less value than the low pair, 9♥ 9♠. However, after focusing your attention on this, be sure to check whether there is any higher-ranking option also available. Do not miss the open-ended 4-card straight, T♣ Q♥ J♥ 9♥ (or T♣ Q♥ J♥ 9♠).

14.   8♦ 9♠ 4♥ Q♥ T♥. Principle # 8 (b) says that *QT* always has less value than a 3-card flush of which it is a part. There are no exceptions to this rule. Q♥ T♥ has less value than 4♥ Q♥ T♥. However, Principle # 12 (a) tells us that, when a 3-card flush has only one high card, it is always inferior to a 4-card inside straight with one or more high cards. Prefer 8♦ 9♠ Q♥ T♥ to 4♥ Q♥ T♥.

15.   J♥ J♣ K♥ 5♣ Q♥. The competition in this hand is between the high pair, J♥ J♣, and the 3-card royal, J♥ K♥ Q♥. The two most valuable 3-card royals are *QJT* and *KQJ* and Principle # 13 tells us that both of these are preferable to {KK, QQ, JJ}. Prefer J♥ K♥ Q♥ to J♥ J♣.

16.   A♣ Q♥ T♥ 7♠ 3♦ and A♣ K♥ T♥ 7♠ 3♦. The only difference between these two hands is that the Q♥ T♥ combination in the first is replaced by the K♥ T♥ combination in the second. From Principle # 7 (b), we know that, in general, when there are two unsuited high cards of which one is an ace, hold only the ace. The question in these hands is whether the A♣ by itself has more or less value than Q♥ T♥ or K♥ T♥. From principle # 10 (b), we know that *QT* and *JT* should be preferred to an ace alone. However, from lines 20 and 21 of the strategy table, we see that an ace alone is preferable to *KT*. In the first hand, prefer Q♥ T♥ to A♣. In the second hand, prefer A♣ to K♥ T♥.

17. Q♣ 5♣ T♣ 9♦ J♣. Whenever *QJT* is present in a hand, do not add a fourth flush card to it unless is can form part of a 4-card straight flush (or 4-card royal). In this hand, prefer Q♣ T♣ J♣ to both the 4-card flush, Q♣ 5♣ T♣ J♣, and the 4-card straight, Q♣ T♣ 9♦ J♣.

18. 7♣ 8♣ 3♠ T♥ J♥. Even though *JT* is the most valuable of all combinations of single high card with suited T, it is ALWAYS appropriate in Double Bonus to extend *JT* into a 4-card inside straight when possible. This is the only game we have found this to be the case. Prefer 7♣ 8♣ T♥ J♥ to T♥ J♥.

19. K♠ Q♠ 2♥ 3♥ 4♥ and K♠ Q♠ 3♥ 4♥ 5♥. Here we are looking at two hands that look very similar. In both hands the competition is between K♠ Q♠ and a consecutive 3-card straight flush. However, the 2♥ 3♥ 4♥ in the first hand and the 3♥ 4♥ 5♥ in the second differ in that the potential of 2♥ 3♥ 4♥ to form straights is limited on the down side by its proximity to the ace. 2♥ 3♥ 4♥ is categorized as a SF3 -1, which in general is worth less than K♠ Q♠. In contrast, the potential of 3♥ 4♥ 5♥ to form straights is not constrained and is categorized as a SF3 +0, which is always preferable to two suited high cards. Prefer K♠ Q♠ to 2♥ 3♥ 4♥ in the first hand, but prefer 3♥ 4♥ 5♥ to K♠ Q♠ in the second.

20. K♣ Q♣ T♦ 9♦ 3♣. This looks like an easy choice between K♣ Q♣ T♦ 9♦ and K♣ Q♣. From Principle # 9 (b), we know that a 4-card inside straight with two high cards is preferable to the high cards alone except when the high cards are suited. In this case, K♣ Q♣ is worth more than K♣ Q♣ T♦ 9♦ – but this is not the best combination to hold from this hand.

Players who are very experienced, like Bob Dancer, can look at a hand like this and normally see all the possibilities at a glance. However, players who play Double Bonus less frequently, like Liam W. Daily, normally see a hand like this and begin analyzing it along the lines of the above paragraph. It is natural at the end of a comparison of two alternatives immediately to hold the more valuable of the two and then press **DRAW**. If you are a frequent player of Jacks or Better (or Deuces Wild), identifying inside straights with high cards is something to which you may be accustomed. The fact that there is a 3♣ at the end of this hand may simply not register as having significance. However, with the flush paying 7 in Double Bonus, you need to be aware that a third flush card is often added to 2-card royals such as K♣ Q♣. Principle # 8 (a) says to extend two suited high cards other than *QJ* into 3-card flushes when possible. In this hand, K♣ Q♣ 3♣ has more value than K♣ Q♣ or K♣ Q♣ T♦ 9♦. If you practice on *Bob Dancer Presents WinPoker*, you will be "beeped" and "flashed" that you have made a "major error" when you miss a third flush card like this. Even though it may take many beepings, you eventually "learn" not to miss these 3-card flush alternatives.

5.6. Basic Strategy Practice Sessions for 10/7 and 9/7

5.6.1. Basic Strategy Practice Session part 1

It is time to test yourself again to see whether you are ready to proceed to Level 4: "Advanced Strategy." As before, the number at the beginning of each line indicates where the correct answer is to be found in the answer column. Even though this is a Level 3 practice session, all answers are "correct" for 10/7 and 9/7; no reversals to the answers will be found in Level 4. This test is repeated on the next page with the difference that the answers are presented in the form of an ordering of the alternative combinations that are available from the opening hand. You may treat the next page as either a separate test or as an aid in achieving the correct answers on this page.

Question						Answer				
17.	A♣	3♣	5♣	7♣	4♣	1.	Q♦	J♦		T♦
4.	6♣	K♦	A♦	3♣	5♣	2.	J♥		K♥	Q♥
20.	J♣	5♣	Q♣	8♣	J♦	3.	A♣			J♣
11.	Q♣	A♦	K♦	J♣	8♣	4.	6♣		3♣	5♣
16.	A♣	J♥	A♥	Q♥	9♥	5.	Q♦		A♦	9♦
3.	A♣	9♦	8♥	Q♦	J♣	6.	9♥	J♥	T♥	
19.	A♣	K♣	7♣	A♦	K♦	7.	2♦	A♣	3♠	5♠
10.	9♦	4♥	J♦	Q♦	4♣	8.		T♣	7♣	Q♣
1.	Q♣	Q♦	J♦	7♦	T♦	9.	Q♣	J♦	K♣	9♠
12.	J♣	Q♣	9♣	K♦	8♣	10.		4♥		4♣
6.	9♥	J♥	T♥	7♦	9♣	11.	Q♣	A♦	K♦	J♣
18.	T♠	Q♦	J♦	9♦	T♥	12.	J♣		9♣	8♣
15.	A♣	Q♣	J♣	T♣	J♥	13.	6♣		5♣	J♣
2.	J♥	K♦	K♥	T♣	Q♥	14.	J♥		Q♠	T♠
8.	8♥	T♣	7♣	K♦	Q♣	15.		J♠		J♥
5.	Q♦	8♥	A♦	T♣	9♦	16.	A♣		A♥	
13.	6♣	9♦	5♣	8♣	J♣	17.	A♣		5♣	4♣
7.	2♦	A♣	3♠	5♠	7♠	18.	T♠ Q♦ J♦ 9♦ or Q♦ J♦ 9♦ T♥			
14.	5♠	J♥	6♣	Q♠	T♠	19.	A♣ K♣ A♦ K♦ in 10/7 A♣ A♦ in 9/7			
9.	Q♣	J♦	K♣	5♣	9♠	20.	J♣ J♦ in 10/7 J♣ 5♣ Q♣ 8♣ in 9/7			

5.6.2. Basic Strategy Practice Session part 2

This test is a repetition of the previous with the difference that you are required to identify the important hand types and place them in priority order. There may up to four different hand types contained in the overall hand. The relative rankings of the combinations can be determined from the Basic Strategy table. Because ST4i 3hi is expressed in the strategy table as "AHHT, KQJ9," and ST4i 4hi as "AKQJ," we use these latter representations in the answers below.

	Question						Answer
17.	A♣	3♠	5♣	7♠	4♣	1.	*QJT* > QQ > FL4 2hi
4.	6♣	K♦	A♦	3♣	5♣	2.	*KQJ* > KK > ST4 non-inside
20.	J♣	5♣	Q♣	8♣	J♦	3.	*AH* > ST4i 2hi
11.	Q♣	A♦	K♦	J♣	8♣	4.	SF3 -1 > *AH*
16.	A♣	J♥	A♥	Q♥	9♥	5.	FL3 2hi > *AH* > ST4i 1hi
3.	A♣	9♦	8♥	Q♦	J♣	6.	SF3 +1 > low pair [55 – TT] > ST4i 1hi
19.	A♣	K♣	7♣	A♦	K♦	7.	ST4i 1hi > SF3 -2 > A
10.	9♦	4♥	J♦	Q♦	4♣	8.	*QTx* > *QT* or KQ
1.	Q♠	Q♦	J♦	7♦	T♦	9.	KQJ9 > FL3 2hi > *KH*
12.	J♣	Q♠	9♣	K♦	8♣	10.	low pair [22 – 44] > SF3 +1 > *QJ*
6.	9♥	J♥	T♥	7♦	9♣	11.	AKQJ > SF3 +0 > *QJ*
18.	T♠	Q♦	J♦	9♦	T♥	12.	SF3 +0 > KQJ9 > ST4i 2hi
15.	A♠	Q♠	J♠	T♣	J♥	13.	FL3 1hi > J > ST4i 0hi
2.	J♥	K♦	K♥	T♣	Q♥	14.	QJT > QJ > *QTx* > *QT*
8.	8♥	T♣	7♣	K♦	Q♣	15.	JJ > *AHH*
5.	Q♦	8♥	A♦	T♣	9♦	16.	AA > FL4 3hi > *AHH*
13.	6♣	9♦	5♣	8♠	J♣	17.	SF3 -1 > ST4i 1hi > A > ST4i 0hi
7.	2♦	A♣	3♠	5♠	7♠	18.	ST4 non-inside > SF3 +1 or low pair [55 – TT]
14.	5♠	J♥	6♣	Q♠	T♠	19.	two pair > AA in 10/7 AA > two pair in 9/7
9.	Q♣	J♦	K♣	5♣	9♠	20.	JJ > FL4 2hi > SF3 +0 in 10/7 FL4 2hi > JJ > SF3 +0 in 9/7

Chapter 6

Level 4: "Advanced Strategy" for 10/7 and 9/7 Double Bonus

6.1. Additional Instructions and Notation for Level 4

6.1.1. Main and Secondary References

In any strategy, there can only be one main reference to a hand option. If there were more than one, you wouldn't know which to use. All main references are outside of parentheses. All main references are ranked identically in both the Advanced Strategy table and the Basic Strategy table.

In the Advanced Strategy table, there may also be secondary references. These secondary references are distinguished by being inside curved parentheses. They represent special penalty-card situations (discussed below) in which the normal ranking of the hand options is changed. These secondary references always occur above the primary reference and they are relevant only to the hand type preceding the parentheses.

When reading a strategy table, always hold the hand option whose main reference is highest on the strategy list, unless it is accompanied by an instruction in parentheses on the same line of strategy to hold one of the alternative lower-ranking hand options. Players who read the strategy from the bottom up are cautioned always to continue up until the last hand option is reached. For example, if you are dealt A♣ T♠ 8♥ 7♠ 6♠, you have three alternatives: the ST4i 0hi, T♠ 8♥ 7♠ 6♠; the SF3 -2, T♠ 7♠ 6♠; and the A♣. If you read the Advanced Strategy table from the bottom up, you will first see the ST4i 0hi on line 23. Above this on line 20 is the ace. This does not automatically mean that, because SF3 -2 is even higher, it must therefore be preferable. There is actually a secondary reference in parentheses to an ace on line 17 in which the main reference to SF3 -2 appears. This secondary reference identifies an oddball situation in which an ace is preferable to a SF3 -2. This hand happens to be such a situation.

6.1.2. Penalty Cards

Many players have difficulty understanding "penalty cards." A penalty card is one of the original five dealt cards in the hand that is usually (but not always) discarded and whose presence affects the value of one or more of the alternative card combinations that may be held from the hand. To try and put some meaning into this definition, here are some examples.

In the previous section, we looked at the hand A♣ T♠ 8♥ 7♠ 6♠ and identified the two primary alternatives as the SF3 -2, T♠ 7♠ 6♠, and the A♣ by itself. The primary reference to SF3 -2 is on line 17 of the Advanced Strategy table, while the primary reference to an ace is on line 20. Although this means that there is a general presumption that the SF3 -2 has more value than the ace, line 17 includes the following exception:

SF3 -2 (< A when sp)

This tells us that SF3 -2 has less value than an ace when the SF3 -2 has a straight penalty (sp). In order to complete a straight, the T♠ 7♠ 6♠ requires both a 9 and an 8. However, since the original five cards contain the 8♥, there are only three rather than four 8s remaining in the pack. This reduces the possibility that the T♠ 7♠ 6♠ will end up as a completed straight. The 8♥ is a straight penalty to the T♠ 7♠ 6♠ and makes the SF3 -2 of less value than the A♣.

Sometimes, a penalty card condition specifies a particular rank of card. For example, on line 19 we have,

KH (< AKH when 9p)

Principle # 7 (a) tells us that, when three high cards of different suits are dealt including an ace, the ace should be discarded. The above condition gives an exception to this. When there is a penalty to the KH in the form of a 9, AKH has more value than KH. Notice that it is only a 9 that is relevant here. Any other straight penalty would also penalize the AKH. In the hand A♥ K♦ J♠ 9♦ 6♥, prefer A♥ K♦ J♠ to K♦ J♠ because of the 9 penalty.

When the rank of a penalty card needs to be specified, it is specified as, for example, a 9p rather than a 9 sp. Although, such penalties will normally be straight penalties, we will find later that there are situations in which a specified rank of penalty card may be other than a straight penalty.

Straight penalties may be "internal," "external," or "at the extreme." In the hand Q♠ J♥ T♥ 8♦ 7♥, the 8♦ is a straight penalty that is internal to the SF3 -1, J♥ T♥ 7♥. However, in the hand Q♦ J♠ T♥ 8♥ 7♥, the J♠ is a straight penalty that is external to the SF3 -1, T♥ 8♥ 7♥. In the hand A♣ J♥ T♥ 7♦ 3♥, the A♣ and the 7♦ are both straight penalties to the J♥ T♥ that are at the extreme in the sense that they are as far removed from the J♥ T♥ as it is possible to be while still being straight penalties.

Straight penalties may also be specified as high-card straight penalties, hsp, and low straight penalties, lsp. The only time a high-card straight penalty is relevant to strategy is in 10/7/80. Compare the two hands, 7♦ 7♥ 8♥ 9♥ J♣ and 7♦ 7♥ 8♥ 9♥ 5♣. In both hands, there is the low pair, 7♦ 7♥, and the SF3 +0, 7♥ 8♥ 9♥. Also, there is a straight penalty to the SF3 +0 in both hands in the form of the J♣ in the first hand and the 5♣ in the second. In both cases, the prospects of 7♥ 8♥ 9♥ ending up as a completed straight are penalized by an equal amount. However, holding 7♥ 8♥ 9♥ has less value when the straight penalty is the J♣ than when it is the 5♣ because the prospects that the final hand will be a high pair is reduced when the J♣ no longer remains in the pack. In 10/7/80, this difference is sufficient to make the 7♦ 7♥ the preferred play in the first hand and the 7♥ 8♥ 9♥ the preferred play in the second.

Low straight penalties are important considerations when deciding whether to hold a single ace or two unsuited high cards including the ace – namely AK, AQ, or AJ. Low straight penalties are always 2s, 3s, 4s, or 5s and refer to the potential of an ace to become an A-low straight. For example, in the hand A♦ Q♥ 8♦ 7♣ 5♠, the 5♠ is a low straight penalty to the A♦ because it reduces the possibility that holding the A♦ by itself will end up as the completed straight, A2345.

On line 20, we have the complicated penalty card condition,

A (< AH when both fp and lsp, except...)

Here we see a reference to both a low straight penalty and a flush penalty, fp. In the previous hand we were considering, A♦ Q♥ 8♦ 7♣ 5♠, the value of the A♦ is not only penalized by the low straight penalty, the 5♠, it is also penalized by the presence in the hand of the 8♦. Because the 8♦ is of the same suit as the A♦, it is a flush penalty to the A♦. The presence of the 8♦ in the original five cards reduces the number of diamonds remaining in the pack from 12 to 11, and therefore reduces the potential for the A♦ to end up as a flush (the reduction from 12 to 11 in the number of diamonds remaining in the pack actually reduces the probability of a flush by one third).

In 10/7/80, there is a reference to a straight flush penalty, sfp,

A (< *KT* with no 9p and when sfp to A)

In the hand A♥ K♦ T♦ 8♠ 5♥, the 5♥ is a straight flush penalty to the ace. As well as penalizing the potential of the A♥ to become a flush or an A2345 straight, it eliminates the possibility that the A♥ may become a straight flush.

You may have noticed in the discussion that we use the term "pack" or "remaining pack" to refer to the 47 cards that remain after the initial 5 cards are dealt. This is to distinguish it from the original "deck" of 52 cards

6.1.3. "When" versus "With"

In all of the references in the above section, the word "when" is used in parentheses. The word "when" is used for penalty-card considerations that refer to the hand option preceding the parentheses. For example, in the first reference to a penalty card condition above, "SF3 -2 (< A when sp)," the "when" means that the straight penalty is referring to the SF3 -2 rather than the ace.

We use the word "with" for penalty-card considerations that refer to the hand option within the parentheses. For example, line 18 of the Advanced Strategy states that,

FL3 1hi (< KH with no sp)

The use of "with" means that the "with no sp" condition is referring to the KH within the parentheses rather than the FL3 1hi outside the parentheses.

To make it easier to distinguish "when" from "with", you may find the following mnemonic device to be useful. Notice that "when" contains the letter "e" (which begins the word "external"), while "with" contains the letter "i" (which begins the word "internal"). "When" generally refers to combinations external to the parentheses, while "with" generally refers to combinations internal to the parentheses. While this mnemonic device doesn't always provide a unique answer when there are multiple brackets, it does work perfectly in the vast majority of cases.

6.1.4. Square Brackets and Curved Brackets

The Level 4 strategies include both square brackets and curved brackets. Square brackets are used to define boundaries on the hand type preceding them. For example, low pairs are qualified as being either [22 – 44] or [55 – TT].

Curved brackets are used to represent exceptions that arise owing to penalty cards such as those illustrated above. It is important to remember that all penalty card situations given in curved brackets refer to the hand type at the beginning of the strategy line as defined or restricted by any square brackets.

It is occasionally necessary to have a third type of brackets to avoid the confusion that can occur when there is a need to stack up brackets. We use curlicue brackets for this purpose. For example, on line 17 of the Advanced Strategy table, we have the condition,

SF3 -2 (< J ... provided no 9p+8p, {or 9p+7p in 9/7})

We have also chosen to use curlicue brackets when we speak of high pairs other than aces, {KK, QQ, JJ}, even though it isn't strictly necessary.

6.2. Advanced Strategy Table for 10/7 and 9/7 Double Bonus

Select the hand option that appears highest in the following list:

1:    RF5; SF5; 4-OF-A-KIND

2:    RF4 > FL5 and ST5 > SF4 any

3:    AAA > FULL HOUSE > 3-OF-A-KIND others

4:    TWO PAIR > AA in 10/7, but TWO PAIR < AA in 9/7

5a*:   *QJT* > FL4 all > RF3 others

5b*:   *KQJ*, *QJT* > KK, QQ, JJ > RF3 others

5c*:   FL4 3hi (also 2hi in 9/7) > KK, QQ, JJ > FL4 others

6:    ST4 non-inside [2345 – KQJT]

7:    low pair [22 – 44] > SF3 +1 [*JT9*, *QJ9*] > low pair [55 – TT]

8:    AKQJ > SF3 +0

9:    AHHT, KQJ9

10:    *QJ*

11:    FL3 2 hi (< *KH* with no sp)

12:    *KH* (*KQ* < SF3 -1 with T-hi)

13:    SF3 -1 (< *AH* when sp) (< ST4i 2hi when internal sp) (when *AJ* "Q98", hold *AJ*)

14:    *AH*

15:    KQJ; ST4i 2hi > ST4i 1hi

16:    QJT > QJ, *JT*, *QT*   (*JT* < *JTx* when two sp, except Ap+7p)

                                (*QT* < SF3-2 with 9-hi)

                                (*QT* always < *QTx*) (*QT* < FL3 1hi when two sp, except Ap+8p)

17:    SF3 -2 (< A when sp) (< J when sp unsuited with J, provided no 9p+8p, {or 9p+7p in 9/7})

                      (in 10/7 only, SF3 -2 [6hi] with sp < J even when sp suited with J)

18:    FL3 1hi (< KH with no sp)

19:    KH (< AKH when 9p)

20:    A (< AH when both fp and lsp, except when Tp unsuited with A)**

21:    *KT*

22:    K, Q, J

23:    ST4i 0hi > FL3 0hi

24:    five new cards

*   Lines 5a, 5b, and 5c cover those situations in which a hand contains any two of the three combinations: {KK, QQ, JJ}, FL4, and RF3. If all three are present, use the following rule:

        "If the RF3 is *QJT*, hold *QJT*. If the RF3 is other than *QJT*, the preferred combination is either {KK, QQ, JJ} or FL4, and can be determined from line 5c alone."

**   In 9/7 only: A (< AH when Tp suited with A and no lsp). This exception has minimal financial significance and is included here for the sake of completeness.

6.3. Exceptions to Basic Strategy for 10/7 and 9/7

Exception # 1 (a) line 11:   FL3 2hi (< *KH* with no sp)

Exception # 1 (b) line 18:   FL3 1hi (< KH with no sp)

Although these two penalty card condition are quite far apart on the strategy table, we are considering them together because they have so much in common.

General Principles # 8 (a) says that two suited high cards other than *QJ* should be extended into 3-card flushes when possible. Exception # 1 (a) identifies an exception to this principle. When *KH* is free of any straight penalty, it should NOT be extended into a 3-card flush. Here are some examples of Exception # 1 (a):

from K♣ J♣ T♦ 7♦ 5♣	prefer	K♣ J♣ 5♣ to	K♣ J♣
from K♣ J♣ 7♣ 6♦ 3♠	prefer	K♣ J♣ to	K♣ J♣ 7♣
from K♥ Q♥ 9♦ 6♦ 2♥	prefer	K♥ Q♥ 2♥ to	K♥ Q♥
from A♦ K♣ J♣ 6♦ 5♣	prefer	K♣ J♣ 5♣ to	K♣ J♣

However, from K♥ Q♥ A♣ 9♥ 7♦, be sure to hold the SF3 +0, K♥ Q♥ 9♥.

Exception # 1 (b) is very similar to Exception # 1 (a) except that it is concerned with KH unsuited and a 3-card flush with only one high card. There is another important distinction between the two of them. In Exception # 1 (a), the FL3 2hi must contain the *KH* and be of the form *KHx*. In Exception # 1 (b), either high card from KH, or even an ace, may represent the high card in the FL3 1hi. For example, the hand A♦ K♣ J♣ 7♦ 4♦ contains the FL3 1hi in the form of A♦ 7♦ 4♦. Because the A♦ penalizes the K♣ J♣, prefer A♦ 7♦ 4♦ to K♣ J♣. In the hand K♥ Q♦ 9♥ 7♦ 5♥, the K♥ Q♦ is penalized by the 9♥ and the K♥ 9♥ 5♥ should be held. However, if this hand had been K♥ Q♦ 8♥ 7♦ 5♥, there would have been no straight penalty and K♥ Q♦ would have been the preferred combination.

Always be on the lookout for higher-ranking combinations that may be present with a FL3 1hi. For example, a 4-card inside straight with one high card is found on line 15 of the strategy table and is always superior to FL3 1hi, which is found on line 18. In the hand K♣ J♦ 9♣ 8♣ 7♣, there is the FL3 1hi, K♣ 8♣ 7♣, and the ST4i 1hi, J♦ 9♣ 8♣ 7♣. Prefer J♦ 9♣ 8♣ 7♣ to K♣ 8♣ 7♣.

Although a 3-card flush with one high card is below *QT* and *JT* on the strategy table, we will see a little later that there are some exceptions.

Exception # 2 line 12:   *KQ* (< SF3 -1 with Thi)

It is important to recognize that this exception applies to *KQ* and not *KJ*. For example, in the hand K♥ Q♥ T♣ 8♣ 7♣, this rule says to prefer T♣ 8♣ 7♣ to K♥ Q♥.

However, this rule does not apply to the hand K♥ J♥ T♣ 8♣ 7♣, where K♥ J♥ is preferable to T♣ 9♣ 7♣. There is no difference in the value of K♥ Q♥ in the first hand and K♥ J♥ in the second; the T♣ penalizes each of them equally. The difference in these two hands comes from the fact that the straight potential of T♣ 9♣ 7♣ is not penalized when the K♥ is accompanied by the Q♥, but is penalized when the K♥ is accompanied by the J♥.

It is only SF3 -1 with T-high that is preferable to *KQ*. Although a SF3 -1 with 9-high would also penalizes *KH*, a 9 represents a straight penalty at the extreme and causes less damage to *KH* than does a T.

Exception # 3 (a) line 13:   SF3 -1 (< *AH* when sp)

It is sometimes easy for inexperienced players to miss the implication of the fact that an ace can act as both the "highest" and the "lowest" card in the deck. For example, in the hand A♥ J♥ 2♦ 3♦ 5♦, it is natural to see both the A♥ and the J♣ as high cards with their potential to make up an AKQJT straight or royal. However, in its function as the "lowest" card in the deck, the ace also penalizes the potential of 2♦ 3♦ 5♦ to become an A2345 straight. Although the hands A♥ J♥ 2♦ 3♦ 5♦ and A♥ J♥ 3♦ 4♦ 6♦ look very similar, it is only the first of them in which the A♥ is a straight penalty to the SF3 -1. The 2♦ 3♦ 5♦ has less value than the A♥ J♥ while the 3♦ 4♦ 6♦ has more value.

As well as SF3 -1 [2-low] being penalized by *AH*, SF3 -1 [T-high] is penalized when in the company of *AJ*. From A♣ J♣ T♣ 9♣ 7♣, prefer A♣ J♣ to T♣ 9♣ 7♣. Although this hand also contains a 4-card inside straight with one high card, both SF3 -1 and *AH* are always more valuable than an inside straight with one high card.

The above examples have been of SF3 -1 that have one inside and no high cards. The other type of SF3 -1 has two insides and one high card. In the hand A♦ Q♦ J♣ 9♣ 7♣, the J♣ 9♣ 7♣ is a SF3 -1 whose straight potential is not penalized by the A♦ or Q♦. In this hand, prefer J♣ 9♣ 7♣ to A♦ Q♦.

Exception # 3 (b) line 13:   SF3 -1 (< ST4i 2hi when internal sp)

Consider the two hands, Q♥ J♣ T♣ 8♣ 7♣ and Q♥ J♣ T♣ 8♦ 7♣. In both cases, there is a SF3 -1 and a ST4i 2hi. In the first case, we have T♣ 8♣ 7♣ and Q♥ J♣ T♣ 8♣. In the second case, we have J♣ T♣ 8♣ and Q♥ J♣ T♣ 8♦. Although the   SF3 -1s in both hands have a straight penalty, there is an important difference.

In the first case, T♣ 8♣ 7♣ is penalized by the presence of the J♣. However, the J♣ is an "external" straight penalty to T♣ 8♣ 7♣. Since Exception # 3 (b) specifically states that the straight penalty must be "internal," SF3 -1 remains superior to ST4i 2hi despite the straight penalty. Prefer T♣ 8♣ 7♣ to Q♥ J♣ T♣ 8♣.

In the second case, J♣ T♣ 7♣ is penalized by the 8♦, which is "internal" to the J♣ T♣ 7♣. In this case, prefer Q♥ J♣ T♣ 8♦ to J♣ T♣ 7♣.

This rule applies only when the inside straight has two high cards. In the hand Q♥ T♦ 9♥ 8♥ 5♣, the Q♥ 9♥ 8♥ is superior to Q♥ T♦ 9♥ 8♥ despite the internal T straight penalty because the inside straight only has one high card. However, in the hand Q♥ J♦ 9♥ 8♥ 5♣ where the T♦ has been changed to the J♦, the Q♥ 9♥ 8♥ has less value than Q♥ J♦ 9♥ 8♥ where the inside straight has two high cards.

Exception # 3 (c) line 13:   SF3 -1 (when *AJ* "Q98" hold *AJ*)

In the hand A♣ Q♦ J♣ 9♦ 8♦, the A♣ J♣ is in competition with both the SF3 -1, Q♦ 9♦ 8♦, and the ST4i 2hi, Q♦ J♣ 9♦ 8♦. Exceptions # 3 (a) would lead us to hold A♣ J♣ rather than Q♦ 9♦ 8♦, while Exception # 3 (b) would lead us to hold Q♦ J♣ 9♦ 8♦ rather than Q♦ 9♦ 8♦. Exception # 3 (c) instructs us to prefer A♣ J♣ to Q♦ J♣ 9♦ 8♦ in this situation. In the Advanced Strategy table, *AH* appears on line 14, while ST4i 2hi appears on line 15. There is no secondary reference on line 14 to *AH* ever being less valuable than ST4i 2hi.

Exception # 4 (a) line 16:   *JT* (< *JTx* when two sp, except Ap+7p)

JT is usually more valuable than *JTx*. It is only when it is crippled by any of the following combinations that *JTx* is held: A9, A8, K8, K7, or Q7. In all cases, both of the cards in these combinations are close enough to be part of a straight with *JT* – but not in the same straight. For example, form A♣ J♦ T♦ 8♣ 5♦, prefer J♦ T♦ 5♦ to J♦ T♦ because the J♦ T♦ is penalized by the two straight penalties, A♣ and 8♣.

It is only when both straight penalties are at the extreme in the form of Ap+7p that the *JT* remains superior to *JTx*. In the hand A♦ J♥ T♥ 7♣ 4♥, prefer J♥ T♥ to J♥ T♥ 4♥.

In the following two hands, K♥ J♣ T♣ 9♦ 4♣ and Q♥ J♣ T♣ 8♦ 4♣, the J♣ T♣ has two straight penalties and has less value than J♣ T♣ 4♣. However, when the two straight penalties are K9 or Q8, a higher-ranking 4-card inside straight with two high cards is created. From K♥ J♣ T♣ 9♦ 4♣, prefer K♥ J♣ T♣ 9♦ to J♣ T♣ 4♣. From Q♥ J♣ T♣ 8♦ 4♣, prefer Q♥ J♣ T♣ 8♦ to J♣ T♣ 4♣.

It is important to note that Exception # 4 (a) only applies to FL3 1hi of which *JT* is a part. *JT* is always preferable to a FL3 1hi of which it not a part (and which is therefore of a different suit). In a hand such as K♣ J♦ T♦ 8♣ 4♣, the J♦ T♦ is the preferred combination.

Exception # 4 (b) line 16:   *QT* (< FL3 1 hi when two sp, except Ap+8p)

QT is usually more valuable than FL3 1hi combinations of which it is not a part. It is only when there are two separate straight penalties other than at the extreme (which means other than Ap+8p) that FL3 1hi is preferable to *QT*. There are only two FL3 1hi that satisfy this condition without creating a higher-ranking 4-card inside straight with two high cards. These are of the form *A9x* and *K8x*. For example, from A♦ Q♥ T♥ 9♦ 4♦, prefer A♦ 9♦ 4♦ to Q♥ T♥.

Line 16 of the Advanced Strategy table includes the condition that was present in the Basic Strategy table, namely: "*QT* (always < *QTx*)." There are no exceptions to this condition. Exception # 4 (b) applies to FL3 1hi of which *QT* is not a part.

Exception # 4 (c) line 16: *QT* (< SF3 -2 with 9hi)

It is not possible for *QT* to interfere with the straight potential of a SF3 -2 because *QT* only exists outside the boundaries of any SF3 -2. However, it is possible for a SF3 -2 to interfere with *QT*. Any SF3 -2 that is 9-high or 8-high would include a straight penalty to *QT*. Exception # 4 (c) identifies only a SF3 -2 [9-high] as being more valuable than *QT*. The reason for this is that that a 9 interferes with both K-high and Q-high straights while an 8 only interferes with only Q-high straights. A 9p is more poisonous to the value of *QT* than is an 8p.

When *QT* and SF3 -2 [9-high] are together in the same hand, there is one situation in which neither the *QT* nor the SF3 -2 [9-high] is the preferred combination. In the hand Q♥ T♥ 9♠ 8♠ 5♠, the preferred play is the ST4i 1hi, Q♥ T♥ 9♠ 8♠, not 9♠ 8♠ 5♠. We could modify the penalty card condition to:

QT (< SF3 -2 [**975** or **965**])

The reason for not choosing to express the condition this way is, first, to keep it as simple as possible, and, second, experienced players when comparing two options learn always to be on the lookout for third, higher-ranking options.

Exception # 5 (a) line 17: SF3 -2 (< A when sp)

In the hand A♥ T♣ 8♣ 6♣ 4♦, the T♣ 8♣ 6♣ is a SF3 -2 that is free of any straight interference and is more valuable than the A♥. However, in the hand A♦ 7♣ 6♣ 4♣ 3♣, the 7♣ 6♣ 3♣ is penalized by the 4♣ and has less value than the A♦. Even if the straight penalty to the SF3 -2 is suited with the ace (and therefore acts as a flush penalty to the ace), the ace is more valuable than the penalized SF3 -2.

This is one of the easier penalty card conditions in Double Bonus. Some readers who are not familiar with our notation may be confused by whether the straight penalty in the condition refers to the SF3 -2 or the A. Remember the distinction that was made between the use of "when" and "with" at the beginning of this chapter. "When" refers to the combination that is outside (or external) to the parentheses, while "with" refers to the combination that is inside the parentheses. The "when" in the above condition is referring to the SF3 -2.

Exception # 5 (b) line 17:

SF3-2 (< J when sp unsuited with J, provided no 9p+8p {or 9p+7p in 9/7})

In games of Jacks or Better, the most valuable high card in the deck is the J because of its wide scope to expand both downwards and upwards into straights. Many students are surprised to learn that the A and the K are the least valuable of the high cards since they both only have two straight potentials, AKQJT and A2345 for an A, and AKQJT and KQJT9 for a K. In Double Bonus, the high payout on quad aces raises the value of the ace to above that of the J. When we compare Exceptions # 5 (a) and 5 (b), we see that the conditions under which a J is more valuable than a SF3 -2 are more restrictive than for an ace.

For a J to have more value than a SF3 -2, there must be a straight penalty to the SF3 -2, but this must not be suited with the J (except in condition 5 (c) below). Also, the SF3 -2 together with the remaining card in the hand must not include both a 9p and an 8p (or a 9p and a 7p in 9/7). It is not necessary that the 9p and the 8p should both be part of the SF3 -2. For example, in the hand J♣ 9♦ 8♦ 6♠ 5♦, the 9p and 8p are part of the SF3 -2, while in the hand J♣ 9♦ 8♠ 6♦ 5♦, only the 9p is a part.

You may be wondering why a Tp is not included. The reason is that it is not possible to have a hand that contains a J together with a penalized T-high SF3 -2 without creating a 4-card inside straight with one high card. Whenever you are looking at a hand that includes a J with two straight penalties, always be on the lookout for a higher-ranking 4-card inside straight that includes the J.

Here are some examples:

from	hold	why
J♣ 8♦ 7♠ 6♦ 4♦	J♣	J♣ has no fp; 8p+7p is insufficient straight interference
J♥ 7♣ 5♣ 4♥ 3♣	7♣ 5♣ 3♣	the sp to SF3 -1 is suited with the J
J♦ 9♣ 8♣ 6♥ 5♣	9♣ 8♣ 5♣	there is a 9p+8p to the J
J♦ 9♥ 8♥ 7♣ 5♥	J♦ 9♥ 8♥ 7♣	ST4i 1hi is always more valuable than SF3 -2
J♥ 9♠ 7♠ 6♣ 5♠	10/7: J♥	9p+7p is NOT sufficient in to "kill" the J in10/7
	9/7: 9♠ 7♠ 5♠	9p+7p is sufficient to "kill" the J in 9/7
J♠ 9♦ 7♦ 6♠ 5♦	9♦ 7♦ 5♦	the sp is suited with the J; the 9p+7p exception in 9/7 only applies when the sp is unsuited with the J.

Exception # 5 (c) line 17:

In 10/7 only, SF3 -2 [6-hi] with sp < J even when sp suited with J

A SF3 -2 with 6-high is the only possible SF3 -2 that does not provide any straight interference to a J. In 10/7 only, a J is slightly more valuable than SF3 -2 [6-high] that has a straight penalty suited with the J. In the hand J♥ 6♣ 4♣ 3♥ 2♣, the J♣ is only worth a tenth of a cent more than 6♣ 4♣ 2♣ in 10/7, but seven-tenths of a cent less in 9/7.

This is a special case related to Exception to # 5 (b) that has very little financial significance. We include it for the sake of completeness. We cannot fault you if you decide never to hold a J in preference to a SF3 -2 that has a sp suited with the J.

Exception # 6 line 19: KH (< AKQ, AKJ when 9p)

Many experienced Double Bonus players know that, because of the 9p in a hand like A♦ K♣ Q♦ 9♠ 5♥, they can earn an extra tenth of a cent by preferring A♦ K♣ Q♦ to K♣ Q♦. Since this is such a small amount, some feel that it is not worth bothering with. They prefer to stick to the General Principle that is common to both Jacks or Better and Double Bonus that, when there are three high cards of different suits of which one is an ace, discard the ace. The authors always play the option with the highest expected return, even if there is only a tenth of a cent in it. This penalty card condition is easy to recognize.

It is important when comparing two hand options to check that you are not missing a third or even fourth. For example, if you look at the hand 3♥ K♠ J♦ A♥ 9♥, and think, "this is just one of those AKH9 hands," you are paying a high price in pursuit of the tenth of one cent. How about the 3-card flush, 3♥ A♥ 9♥? This is found on line 18 of the strategy table, ahead of KH and AKH on line 19. The amount by which 3♥ A♥ 9♥ is of greater value than K♠ J♦ A♥ is 60 times as great as the amount by which K♠ J♦ A♥ is of greater value than K♠ J♦ with a 9p.

It is important to note that Exception # 6 applies only to AKH. In the hand A♥ Q♦ J♣ 9♥ 5♠, the Q♦ J♣ is more valuable than A♥ Q♦ J♣ even when it has a 9p.

Exception # 7 line 20:

A (< AH when both fp and lsp, except when Tp unsuited with A)

This is probably the most difficult penalty-card situation in Double Bonus. You need to look for the presence of two separate penalty cards and the absence of another one. Looking for the absence of something may not come easily to some people. Even when all three of the necessary conditions exist, holding AH is usually less than ½ a cent superior to holding the ace by itself. Some readers may feel that the following is way too difficult to be worth the extra half cent that will sometimes accrue. The authors always work to play these hands correctly. However, we recognize that the mental process of applying this complicated penalty card condition may distract some players from recognizing alternative more valuable hand options. Before beginning the process of deciding whether an ace is more or less valuable than AH, always check the whole hand to see whether there is some other alternative that is more valuable than both.

The first thing to notice about the above penalty card condition is that it takes both a flush penalty and a low straight penalty (which could be a 2, 3, 4, or 5) for the ace ever to be of less value on its own than in combination with another high card. For example, in the hand A♣ Q♦ 9♠ 7♣ 3♥, the A♣ alone is penalized by both the 7♣ and the

3♥, whereas the A♣ Q♦ is not penalized at all. The expected return on A♣ Q♦ is around four tenths of a cent more than on A♣ alone.

The need for there to be both a flush penalty and a low straight penalty is satisfied by a single straight flush penalty (which could be a 2, 3, 4, or 5 of the same suit as the ace). Not only does a straight flush penalty penalize the potential of the ace to become a flush or an A2345 straight, it also eliminates the possibility of the ace becoming a straight flush. In the hand A♦ 5♦ 7♣ 9♠ K♣, the expected return on A♦ K♣ is a little more than four-tenths of a cent greater than on A♣ alone.

It is NOT sufficient for there to be two low straight penalties in the absence of a flush penalty. In the hand A♥ 3♣ 5♦ 7♠ J♦, the A♥ has more value than A♥ J♦ despite being penalized by both the 3♣ and the 5♦. In the event that there were two flush penalties, there would be a higher-ranking 3-card flush with one high card.

The second part of the penalty card condition on line 20 gives an exception in which a lone ace is superior to any AH combination. This exception applies even when there is maximum interference to the ace in the form of both a straight flush penalty and a low straight penalty:

In any hand that includes a T unsuited with the ace, always prefer A to AH.

The reason for this exception is that a T penalizes AH by much more than it penalizes the ace alone, provided it is not suited with the ace. For example, although there is both a flush penalty and a low straight penalty in the hand A♣ J♦ T♠ 6♣ 3♦, the presence of the T♠ hurts the straight potential of the A♣ J♦ combination sufficiently to make the A♣ the preferred alternative.

When considering a T that is unsuited with the ace, it is important to be aware of whether the T is suited with the other high card. If it is, then there may be a *HT* option that is superior to the ace. We know from Principle # 10 (b) that both *QT* and *JT* are preferable to an ace alone. In the hand A♥ Q♦ T♦ 6♥ 5♠, the T is unsuited with the ace. However, although A♥ has more value than A♥ Q♦, both are significantly less valuable than Q♦ T♦. When a T is unsuited with the ace, the only high card that the T may be suited with without creating a third, more valuable option is a K. Here is a summary:

When a hand contains an A plus *KT*, prefer A to AK

When a hand contains an A plus *QT*, prefer *QT* to A

When a hand contains an A plus *JT*, prefer *JT* to A

When a hand contains an A with a T unsuited with either high card, prefer A to AH.

When a hand contains *AT*, the suited T should be treated as you would any other flush penalty, except under one special condition that is covered in a footnote to the Advanced Strategy table and which applies to 9/7 only:

81

In 9/7 only: A (< AH when Tp suited with A and no lsp).

This exception has minimal financial significance and is included here for the sake of completeness.

When going through the procedure of comparing A to AH, it is easy to get caught up in the analysis and miss the possibilities of other higher-ranking combinations that may be present in the hand. Be sure to check all five cards. In particular, there are three hand types that you should be on the lookout for:

   (1)   Watch out for a 3-card straight flush. For example,

       from A♠ Q♥ 9♥ 8♥ 4♠   prefer   Q♥ 9♥ 8♥ to   A♠ Q♥
       from A♠ K♦ T♦ 5♠ 2♠   prefer   A♠ 5♠ 2♠ to   A♠

   (2)   Watch out for a 4-card inside straight with one high card. For example,

       from A♣ J♦ 5♠ 3♦ 2♣   prefer A♣ 5♠ 3♦ 2♣ to A♣ J♦ or A♣
       from A♥ J♣ T♠ 8♥ 7♠   prefer J♣ T♠ 8♥ 7♠ to A♥ or A♥ J♣

   (3)   Watch out for a 3-card flush. For example,

       from A♥ J♦ 8♥ 6♣ 3♥   prefer A♥ 8♥ 3♥ to   A♥ J♦
       from A♥ K♦ 9♥ 7♦ 5♦   prefer K♦ 7♦ 5♦ to   A♥ K♦

6.4. Advanced Strategy Examples for 10/7 and 9/7

As in the previous sets of examples, these hands are presented at random and the order of the cards is sometimes jumbled in a way that makes it harder to recognize all the alternatives. These examples are an important addition to the preceding discussion. They include many situations that straddle more than one of the exceptions listed above.

1.   A♥ J♥ 2♦ 3♦ 4♦ and A♥ J♥ 3♦ 4♦ 6♦. At first glance, the 2♦ 3♦ 4♦ in the first hand looks more valuable than the 3♦ 4♦ 6♦ in the second. However, players who have mastered the Basic Strategy should know that **234** is classified as a SF3 -1 because its downward straight potential is limited by its proximity to the ace. Both 2♦ 3♦ 4♦ and 3♦ 4♦ 6♦ are SF3 -1. From Exception # 3 (a), we know that it is only when SF3 -1 has a straight penalty that it is of less value than **AH**. In its capacity as the "lowest" card in the deck, the A♥ is a straight penalty to 2♦ 3♦ 4♦ but not to 3♦ 4♦ 6♦. In the first hand, prefer A♥ J♥ to 2♦ 3♦ 4♦. In the second hand, prefer 3♦ 4♦ 6♦ to A♥ J♥. Note that, although the first hand includes the 4-card inside straight, A♥ 2♦ 3♦ 4♦, an inside straight with only one high card never has more value than SF3 -1 or two suited high cards.

2.   A♥ 8♥ J♦ 4♦ T♦. Although *JT* is normally more valuable than a 3-card flush of which it is a part, Exception # 4 (a) tells us that it is less valuable when it has two straight penalties other than the two at the extreme, Ap+7p. In this hand, the J♦ T♦ has

two straight penalties, the A♥ and 8♥. Since the 8♥ is not at the extreme, the combined effect of the Ap+8p is to hurt J♦ T♦ sufficiently such that it is better to extend it into J♦ 4♦ T♦.

3. Q♥ 9♦ T♦ K♥ 3♥. The alternatives in this hand are: the 4-card inside straight with two high cards, Q♥ 9♦ T♦ K♥; the two suited high cards, Q♥ K♥; and, last but not least, the 3-card flush, Q♥ K♥ 3♥. We know that an inside straight with two high cards is only preferable to the high cards alone when the high cards are unsuited. In this case, Q♥ K♥ is preferable to Q♥ 9♦ T♦ K♥. However, when you have two suited high cards other than *QJ*, always be on the lookout for a third flush card. *AH* should always be extended into a three card flush when possible, while *KH* should when it has a straight penalty, as per Exception # 1 (a). With both the 9♦ and the T♦ as penalties to Q♥ K♥, hold Q♥ K♥ 3♥.

4. A♥ K♣ 3♦ 4♥ 5♥. Whenever you see an ace accompanied by a cluster of very low cards, check for the possibilities of an A-low 4-card inside straight or an A-low 3-card straight flush. Either option is preferable to an A alone or AH combination. In this hand, there is the inside straight, A♥ 3♦ 4♥ 5♥, and the 3-card straight flush, A♥ 4♥ 5♥. Although Exception # 3 (b) identifies a condition in which SF3 -1 has less value than ST4i 2hi, there are no exceptions to the rule that SF3 -1 is superior to ST4i 1hi. Prefer A♥ 4♥ 5♥ to A♥ 3♦ 4♥ 5♥.

5. J♥ T♣ 7♦ A♦ 3♣. The choice in this hand is between the J♥ A♦ and the A♦ alone. Although the A♦ is penalized by both the 7♦ and the 3♣, the A♦ is "rescued" by the presence of the T♣, which is unsuited with the ace and penalizes the straight potential of the J♥ A♦. Prefer A♦ to J♥ A♦.

6. K♣ J♥ T♦ 9♦ 7♦ and K♣ J♦ T♥ 9♦ 7♦. These two hands are identical except that the suits of the J and T have been switched. Both hands contain the two unsuited high cards, KJ, and the 4-card inside straight with 2 high cards, KJT9. Since the K and J are of different suits, the KJT9 inside straight has more value than the two high cards alone. Both hands also contain a SF3 -1. In the first case, it is T♦ 9♦ 7♦; in the second case, it is J♦ 9♦ 7♦. Exception # 3 (b) tells us that a SF3 -1 with an internal straight penalty is less valuable than a ST4i 2hi. In the first hand, there is no internal straight penalty to T♦ 9♦ 7♦, so prefer T♦ 9♦ 7♦ to K♣ J♥ T♦ 9♦. In the second hand, the J♦ 9♦ 7♦ has the T♥ as an internal straight penalty, so prefer the K♣ J♦ T♥ 9♦ to J♦ 9♦ 7♦.

7. K♥ J♦ 8♥ 2♥ 9♦. This hand is a simple application of Exception # 1 (b). Because the K♥ J♦ is penalized by the 9♦, it has less value than the 3-card flush with one high card, K♥ 8♥ 2♥. If the K♥ in this hand were changed to the Q♥, we would have Q♥ J♦ 8♥ 2♥ 9♦. The preferred combination would now be totally different. QJ unsuited is ALWAYS more valuable than FL3 1hi, but NEVER more valuable than ST4i 2hi. In this second hand, the most valuable combination is therefore Q♥ J♦ 8♥ 9♦, followed by Q♥ J♦, followed by Q♥ 8♥ 2♥.

8. 3♦ A♥ K♦ J♠ 9♦. Players who immediately recognize that A♥ K♦ J♠ is preferable to K♦ J♠ owing to the presence of the 9♦ are to be commended – provided they also recognize that the hand also contains the 3-card flush, 3♦ K♦ 9♦. The combination, A♥ K♦ J♠, is worth a tenth of a cent more than K♦ J♠, but six cents less than, 3♦ K♦ 9♦.

9. 2♠ 3♠ 6♠ A♣ 5♣. This hand contains the SF3 -2, 2♠ 3♠ 6♠, which is penalized by the 5♣. This 5♣ also happens to be a straight flush penalty to the A♣. Despite having a straight flush penalty, the A♣ is preferable to the penalized 2♠ 3♠ 6♠ as per Exception # 5 (a), but it is not the preferred combination from this hand. 2♠ 3♠ A♣ 5♣ is a 4-card inside straight with one high card. As such, it is superior to a single high card or a SF3 -2 (except in some instances discussed in the following chapters when the straight flush pays 80).

10. K♣ 4♥ 6♥ A♠ 9♠. In this hand, the A♠ has both a flush penalty, the 9♠, and a low straight penalty, the 4♥. Since there is no unsuited T, prefer K♣ A♠ to A♠.

11. T♥ Q♥ 5♥ 8♦ 9♠. It is easy in this hand to spot the FL3 1hi, T♥ Q♥ 5♥. We know from the General Principles that *QTx* is always preferable to *QT*. Perhaps harder to spot is the 4-card inside straight with one high card, T♥ Q♥ 8♦ 9♠. ST4i 1hi is on line 15 of the Advanced Strategy table and there are no conditions under which it is ever of less value than FL3 1hi or *QT* (or *JT*). Prefer T♥ Q♥ 8♦ 9♠ to T♥ Q♥ 5♥.

12. 5♣ 4♦ 6♦ J♣ 2♦. In Exception # 5 (b), one of the conditions necessary for a J to be preferable to a SF3 -2 is that the SF3 -2 should be penalized by a card that is not of the same suit as the J. Exception # 5 (c) represents an "exception to the exception." In 10/7 only, the straight penalty may be suited with the J if the SF3 -2 is 6-high. In this hand, the straight penalty is the 5♣, which is of the same suit as the J♣. Therefore, prefer J♣ to 4♦ 6♦ 2♦ in 10/7, but prefer 4♦ 6♦ 2♦ to J♣ in 9/7.

13. 3♠ K♠ J♦ A♥ 9♥ and 3♠ Q♠ J♦ A♥ 9♥. Here are two hands that are identical except that the K♠ in the first hand is replaced by the Q♠ in the second. The first hand is an example of Exception # 6 in which K♠ J♦ A♥ has slightly more value than K♠ J♦ owing to the presence of the 9♥. In the second hand, the Q♠ J♦ is always more valuable than Q♠ J♦ A♥ or the A♥ alone no matter how it is penalized.

14. 3♥ 5♥ A♣ 6♦ 7♥. Exception # 5 (a) is one of the easiest penalty card conditions in Double Bonus. Whenever a SF3 -2 has a straight penalty, it is inferior to an ace. In this hand, the 6♦ penalizes the 3♥ 5♥ 7♥ and makes the A♣ preferable.

15. 2♣ T♥ A♣ J♦ 5♣. Since the A♣ is accompanied by the unsuited T♥, Exception # 7 tells us that the A♣ is preferable to A♣ J♦ even if the ace is penalized by both a flush penalty and a low straight penalty. This does not mean necessarily that you should simply just hold the A♣. We identified three options that you should be on the lookout for when faced with one of these A versus AH situations. These three options are a 3-card flush that includes one of the high cards, a 3-card straight flush, and a

4-card inside straight. This hand also contains the 3-card straight flush, 2♣ A♣ 5♣, which has significantly more value than the A♣ alone.

16   T♣ A♥ Q♣ 9♥ 5♥. This hand contains the 3-card flush with one high card, the A♥ 9♥ 5♥, and a single high card with a suited T, the T♣ Q♣. From Exception # 4 (b), we know that *QT* has less value than a FL3 1hi of a different suit when there are two straight penalties to the *QT* other than Ap+8p. Since the two straight penalties in this hand are Ap+9p, prefer A♥ 9♥ 5♥ to T♣ Q♣.

17.   9♦ 7♦ Q♣ T♣ 5♦. Exception # 4 (c) gives the only situation in which *QT* has less value than SF3 -2, and that is when the SF3 -2 is 9-high. In this hand, 9♦ 7♦ 5♦ is preferable to Q♣ T♣ because the 9♦ penalizes the Q♣ T♣. Although an 8-high SF3 -2 would also give straight interference to *QT*, an 8p is at the extreme and does not harm *QT* sufficiently to make it less valuable than SF3 -2. Note if this hand were changed from 9♦ 7♦ Q♣ T♣ 5♦ to 9♦ 8♦ Q♣ T♣ 5♦, the 9♦ 8♦ 5♦ would still has more value than Q♣ T♣, BUT both would be inferior to the ST4i 1hi, 9♦ 8♦ Q♣ T♣.

18.   K♦ J♣ 4♦ 8♦ T♣. We know from Exception # 1 (b) that KH has less value than FL3 1hi when there is a straight penalty to the KH. While it is true the K♦ 8♦ 5♦ in this hand has more value than K♦ J♣ owing to the T penalty, it is not the correct play. This hand also contains J♣ T♣. In the Advanced Strategy table, *JT* is on line 16 compared to FL3 1hi on line 18. There is no reference in parenthesis on line 16 to any condition in which *JT* is of less value than a FL3 1hi of which it is not a part. Although the J♣ T♣ is penalized by the K♦ and the 8♦, it is the preferred combination in this hand, followed by K♦ 8♦ 5♦, and, finally, K♦ J♣.

19.   A♥ K♦ Q♦ 6♥ 4♦. When there are a number of high cards present in a hand, they can sometimes impair your vision of the low cards. In this hand, one may immediately notice the A♥ K♦ Q♦. Because the K♦ Q♦ are suited, we know they have more value than A♥ K♦ Q♦. However, whenever you have *AH* or *KH* in a hand, always be on the lookout for the possibility of extending them into a 3-card flush. *AHx* is always preferable to *AH*, while *KHx* is preferable to *KH* with a straight penalty. Because the A♥ is a straight penalty to the K♦ Q♦, prefer K♦ Q♦ 4♦ to K♦ Q♦.

20.   Q♥ 9♥ A♦ 8♥ J♦. This hand contains: the SF3 -1, Q♥ 9♥ 8♥; the *AH* combination, A♦ J♦; and the 4-card inside straight with two high cards, Q♥ 9♥ 8♥ J♦. Because Q♥ 9♥ 8♥ has a straight penalty, Exception # 3 (a) would say that A♦ J♦ is superior to Q♥ 9♥ 8♥, while Exception # 3 (b) would say that Q♥ 9♥ 8♥ J♦ is superior. Because of the confusion that this may cause, we have included a specific reference to this hand as Exception # 3 (c). Two suited high cards are always preferable to a 4-card inside straight with two high cards. Prefer A♦ J♦ to Q♥ 9♥ 8♥ J♦.

21.   3♥ 7♥ K♦ J♣ A♥. While it is true that KH is preferable to AKH except when there is a 9p, it is important to spot the presence in this hand of the FL3 1hi, 3♥ 7♥ A♥. We know from Exception # 1 (b) that 3♥ 7♥ A♥ is preferable to K♦ J♣ because the A♥ is a straight penalty to K♦ J♣. If this hand were changed to 3♥ 7♥ K♣ J♣ A♥ with the K and

J of the same suit, it would be covered by Exception # 1 (a). Although K♠ J♠ is still penalized by the A♥, it would not have been appropriate to hold 3♥ 7♥ A♥. When *KH* has a straight penalty, it is only inferior to a FL3 2hi that takes the form of *KHx*.

22. T♥ 7♥ K♣ Q♣ 9♥ and T♥ 7♥ K♣ J♣ 9♥. In both these hands, *KH* is in competition with SF3 -1 [T-high]. Exception # 2 states that *KQ* but not *KJ* is inferior to SF3 -1 [T-high]. The difference between these two hands is that T♥ 7♥ 9♥ is free of any straight interference from K♣ Q♣ in the first hand. In contrast, T♥ 7♥ 9♥ is penalized by the J♣ in the second. In the first hand, prefer T♥ 7♥ 9♥ to K♣ Q♣. In the second hand, prefer K♣ J♣ to T♥ 7♥ 9♥.

23. 4♣ A♠ J♣ 5♣ 2♥. It is easy to see that the A♠ in this hand is penalized by both a flush penalty and a low straight penalty. However, if you look closely you will see that there is also a 4-card inside straight including the ace contained in the hand. Prefer 4♠ A♠ 5♣ 2♥ to A♠ J♣.

24. J♣ 6♥ 5♥ 7♦ 9♥. This hand contains a SF3 -2, 6♥ 5♥ 9♥, that has a straight penalty, the 7♦, which is unsuited with the J♣. Under these conditions, the J is superior to the SF3 -2 unless the J is penalized by a 9p+8p, or also by a 9p+7p in 9/7. Since there is a 9p+7p to the J in this hand, prefer the 6♥ 5♥ 9♥ to the J♣ in 9/7, but prefer the J♣ to the 6♥ 5♥ 9♥ in 10/7.

25. 6♥ 5♦ A♥ K♦ T♦. Whenever an ace is accompanied by *KT* suited, the ace is always preferable to the AK. Because the T is unsuited with the ace, it "permits" the ace to have both a flush penalty and a low straight penalty and still be preferable to AK. We also know that *KT* is never more valuable than an ace alone (with one exception in 10/7/80). In this hand, the A♥ has more value than A♥ K♦. Before automatically holding the ace alone when accompanied by *KT*, always check to see whether there is another card in the hand of the same suit as the *KT*. In this hand, there is the 5♦ to accompany the K♦ T♦. Hold 5♦ K♦ T♦.

6.5. Advanced Strategy Practice Session for 10/7 and 9/7

This practice session includes hands that are as difficult as any you are likely to come across in 10/7 and 9/7 Double Bonus. When you can get all these correct, you may truly call yourself an expert.

Question						Answer				
17.	J♣	K♦	9♣	T♦	7♣	1.	K♠	A♦		
4.	J♦	8♣	A♥	K♦	6♦	2.	A♥		K♣	Q♦
20.	9♣	5♣	7♥	6♣	J♣	3.	9♣		7♣	5♣
11.	J♥	A♦	3♦	T♣	8♥	4.	J♦		K♦	6♦
16.	K♣	Q♦	A♥	6♦	9♦	5.	A♠	6♠		9♠
3.	9♣	T♦	7♣	5♣	Q♦	6.		T♥		J♥
19.	6♣	3♥	J♥	4♣	2♣	7.	K♣	T♣		5♣
10.	K♣	5♥	T♣	Q♦	9♣	8.			A♦	
1.	K♠	A♦	5♣	8♥	2♦	9.	T♣	8♣		7♣
12.	7♥	6♥	5♦	3♥	A♠	10.	K♣		T♣ Q♦	9♣
6.	7♦	T♥	A♠	5♥	J♥	11.		A♦		
18.	J♣	T♠	A♣	7♠	8♠	12.				A♠
15.	8♦	A♥	T♦	J♦	Q♣	13.	K♦			Q♣
2.	A♥	4♣	K♣	Q♦	9♦	14.	A♦		J♦	
8.	T♣	K♣	A♦	3♠	5♦	15.	8♦		T♦	J♦
5.	A♠	Q♣	6♠	T♣	9♣	16.		Q♦		6♦ 9♦
13.	K♦	6♣	8♦	7♦	Q♣	17.	J♣	K♦	9♣	T♦
7.	K♣	T♣	J♦	5♣	4♠	18.	J♣		A♣	
14.	A♦	8♥	J♦	Q♥	9♥	19.	J♠ in 10/7			
							6♣ 4♣ 2♣ in 9/7			
9.	T♣	8♣	K♦	Q♦	7♣	20.	J♣ in 10/7			
							9♣ 5♣ 6♣ in 9/7			

Chapter 7

Basic Strategy for 10/7/80 Double Bonus

7.1. Introduction to 10/7/80 Double Bonus

Both the authors have a fondness for 10/7 Double Bonus because of its high return and because full mastery of the game requires considerable skill and attentive play. We also love getting quads, particularly when they are aces or the premium 2s, 3s, and 4s. Unfortunately, Liam W. Daily feels a little hard-done-by when we gets a rare straight flush and only receives 250 coins. This is the same payout as a non-premium quad, which you can expect to get almost once an hour. When you have to wait an average of 15 hours to get a straight flush, it would be nice if it paid a little more.

Although the majority of Double Bonus games available pay 250 for a 5-coin straight flush, the version of 10/7 Double Bonus found on Bally GameMaker machines returns 400 for a 5-coin straight flush. This game is normally referred to as 10/7/80 where the 80 represents the single-coin payout on the straight flush. In the last two chapters of this Guide, we refer to the 10/7 and 9/7 games with a 50 payout on the straight flush as 10/7/50 and 9/7/50, respectively, to avoid ambiguity. For ease of reference, we also use the terms "SF-50" and "SF-80" when we are making comparisons that depend only on whether the straight flush pays 50 or 80. There is one potential source of confusion and that is, if you actually play less than maximum coins on 10/7/80, the payout on the straight flush is reduced to 50. Be sure to look at the 5-coin payout schedule.

The increase on the payout on the straight flush from 50 to 80 increases the return from 100.17% to 100.52%. This triples the edge in favor of the player. Liam W. Daily enjoys getting straight flushes much more in this game. Bob Dancer doesn't particularly care about where the extra return comes from. He knows that he will hit a straight flush every 15 hours or so, so the additional $150 he'll receive from playing on a dollar 10/7/80 machine rather than a 10/7/50 machine amounts to an extra $10 per hour. He adds this to the $5 per hour the game pays anyway and adds in an amount for the slot club assuming he plays $3,000 per hour on a dollar machine. (This is a low amount for some of the newer machines that rack up credits quickly and a high amount for the machines that spill coins into the tray every time you get above 400 credits.) A 0.25% slot club, then, would add $7.50 per hour to his expected win. Dancer adds these numbers together to decide where he is going to play today.

If you normally play 10/7/50 but find a 10/7/80 game nearby, move to it. Even if you only know the strategy for 10/7/50, you will be better off playing 10/7/80. You will simply get the extra payout if you hit a straight flush. Playing perfect strategy for 10/7/80 gives a return of 100.52%. However, if you play 10/7/50 strategy, you can still get a return of 100.51%. These returns are very close. You may be wondering whether it is worth the effort to learn the 10/7/80 strategy. The authors feel the need to know because they are not comfortable playing a game in which they are unsure of the preferred play. For example, if you are dealt Q♥ J♥ T♥ 9♥ 8♣, aren't you curious to know whether you should break the straight and go after the higher paying straight flush? If you are dealt J♣ T♣ 9♣ 4♦ 4♥, wouldn't you like to know whether the higher-paying straight flush has made it preferable to hold the SF3 +1 rather than the pair of 4s?

In chapters 2 and 3, we presented Beginner and Recreational Strategies that apply whether the straight flush pays 50 or 80. The critical payouts for these strategies were 7 for a flush and 5 for a straight rather than the payouts on the full house and straight flush. In this chapter, we present Level 3: "Basic Strategy" for 10/7/80. Although fundamentally similar to 10/7/50 strategy, there are sufficient departures to warrant a separate strategy. Chapter 8 presents Level 4: "Advanced Strategy." Together with an appendix, the goal of the Advanced Strategy is to be computer perfect.

7.2. Basic Strategy Table for 10/7/80

Select the hand option that appears highest in the following list:

1:      RF5; SF5; 4-OF-A-KIND

2:      RF4 > FL5, ST5 > SF4 any (except *QJT9*, *JT98* > ST5)

3:      AAA > FULL HOUSE > 3-OF-A-KIND others

4:      TWO PAIR > AA

5a:*   *QJT* > FL4 all > RF3 others

5b:*   *KQJ*, *QJT* > KK, QQ, JJ > RF3 others

5c:*   FL4 3hi > KK, QQ, JJ > FL4 others

6:      ST4 non-inside [2345 – KQJT]

7:      SF3 +1 [*JT9*, *QJ9*] > low pair [22 – TT]

8:      SF3 +0 > AKQJ (except *KH9* < AKQJ)

9:      AHHT, KQJ9

10:     SF3 -1

11:     *QJ*

12:     FL3 2 hi

13:     *KH*

14:     *AH*

15:     KQJ

16:     ST4i 2hi > SF3 -2 > ST4i 1hi

17:     QJT > QJ, *JT*

18:     FL3 1hi [*QTx*] > *QT* > FL3 1hi [others]

19:     KH

20:     A

21:     *KT*

22:     K, Q, J

23:     ST4i 0hi > FL3 0hi

24:     five new cards

*   Lines 5a, 5b, and 5c cover those situations in which a hand contains any two of the three combinations: {KK, QQ, JJ}, FL4, and RF3. If all three are present, use the following rule:

> "If the RF3 is *QJT*, hold *QJT*. If the RF3 is other than *QJT*, the preferred combination is either {KK, QQ, JJ} or FL4, and can be determined from line 5c alone."

7.3. Similarities between SF-50 and SF-80 Basic Strategies

Similarity # 1. When none of the options in a hand has the potential to become a straight flush, the SF-50 and SF-80 strategies are identical.

One of the General Principles of Double Bonus strategy is to prefer a 4-card flush to a 4-card open-ended straight, and prefer both to a low pair. This is a good example of an important rule that applies in 10/7/80 just as much as it applies in 10/7/50. None of these combinations has any potential to become a straight flush and the rule is independent of the payout on the straight flush. For example, if you are dealt the hand 3♣ 4♥ 5♦ 6♥ 6♦, play it identically in SF-50 and SF-80; prefer the 4-card straight, 3♣ 4♥ 5♦ 6♥ (or 3♣ 4♥ 5♦ 6♦) to the low pair, 6♥ 6♦. There are many important decisions like this that are independent of the payout on the straight flush. The following is a random list of illustrations.

(1)   In the hand K♣ Q♦ 9♦ 5♣ 2♦, the alternatives are K♣ Q♦ and Q♦ 9♦ 2♦. Neither has the possibility of becoming a straight flush, so hold Q♦ 9♦ 2♦ just as you would in 10/7/50.

(2)   In the hand Q♦ Q♣ J♣ 7♣ 4♣, Principle # 14 tells us that a 4-card flush must contain three high cards to be superior to {KK, QQ, JJ} in 10/7, but only two high cards in 9/7. Again these combinations are independent of the payout on the straight flush. Since the game with the 80 payout on the straight flush is a 10/7 game, three high cards are needed, so prefer Q♦ Q♣ to Q♣ J♣ 7♣ 4♣.

(3)   In the hand A♥ K♥ 8♥ 6♦ 3♣, the alternatives are A♥ K♥ and A♥ K♥ 8♥. Given that neither has straight flush potential, follow the rule of always extending *AH* into *AHx* when possible.

(4)   In the hand 3♣ 4♦ 5♦ 7♣ T♦, the alternatives are the 4-card inside straight with no high cards, 3♣ 4♦ 5♦ 7♣, and the 3-card flush with no high cards, 4♦ 5♦ T♦. Neither has straight flush potential. Principle # 12 (b) instructs us to "hold a 4-card inside straight with no high cards, or a 3-card flush with no high cards, only if there is absolutely nothing else in the hand worth holding; prefer the inside straight to the 3-card flush." Since there is nothing else worth holding in this hand, hold 3♣ 4♦ 5♦ 7♣ in both SF-50 and SF-80.

(5)   In the hand Q♦ J♣ T♣ 8♥ 5♣, neither Q♦ J♣ T♣ 8♥ nor Q♦ J♣ T♣ has the potential to form a straight flush, so continue to prefer Q♦ J♣ T♣ 8♥ to Q♦ J♣ T♣.

Similarity # 2. When the preferred combination in SF-50 is a SF3 or SF4, it will be the preferred combination in SF-80.

We know from SF-50 strategy that SF3 +1 is superior to a low pair [55 – TT]. For example, from Q♦ J♦ 9♦ 6♣ 6♣, prefer Q♦ J♦ 9♦ to 6♣ 6♣. In SF-80, the value of Q♦ J♦ 9♦ is increased while the value of 6♣ 6♣ is unchanged. Q♦ J♦ 9♦ exceeds the value of 6♣ 6♠ by an even larger margin. Here are a few more random examples to demonstrate this point.

(1)   The General Principle of extending 2-card royals or single high cards into 3-card straight flushes when possible is even stronger in SF-80 than SF-50. In the hand A♣ 7♦ 5♣ T♠ 2♣, continue to prefer A♣ 5♣ 2♣ to A♣ alone.

(2)   In the hand A♣ A♥ 3♥ 4♥ 5♥, you break the A♣ A♥ for the SF4, A♥ 3♥ 4♥ 5♥ whether it is SF-50 or SF-80.

(3)   Given that a SF3 +0 has more value than any two suited high cards in SF-50, this will continue to be the case in SF-80. From 4♣ 5♣ 6♣ J♦ Q♦, continue to prefer 4♣ 5♣ 6♣ to J♦ Q♦

(4)   In the hand Q♥ J♦ T♦ 7♦ 5♠, the value of the SF3 -1, J♦ T♦ 7♦, exceeds the value of Q♥ J♦ T♦ by an even larger margin in SF-80 than in SF-50.

(5)   In the hand K♥ Q♣ 7♦ 5♦ 3♦, the SF3 -2, 7♦ 5♦ 3♦, is preferable to K♥ Q♣ in SF-50 and so is preferable (by a larger amount) in SF-80.

Similarity # 3.   When two cards to a potential straight flush are preferred to a single high card or a combination that has no straight flush potential in SF-50, the preferred combination will remain the same in SF-80.

It is important to remember that all 2-card royal flushes except those including an ace have the potential to form a straight flush. They therefore have greater value in SF-80 than in SF-50. A good example of the above similarity comes from the General Principle that two suited high cards should be preferred to three high cards of mixed suits. From K♣ Q♦ J♣ 7♦ 4♥, the K♣ J♣ is even more valuable than K♣ Q♦ J♣ in SF-80 than it is in SF-50 since K♣ Q♦ J♣ has no straight flush potential. Other examples of this similarity are:

(1)   In the hand Q♣ J♣ 7♣ 6♦ 3♣, the Q♣ J♣ is preferable to Q♣ J♣ 7♣ in SF-50, and so remains preferable in SF-80.

(2)   Although there are situations in Jacks or Better in which it is appropriate to drop the *T* from *KT*, this is never the case in 10/7/50. It will therefore never be the case in 10/7/80.

(3)   In the hand K♥ Q♦ T♦ 6♣ 3♠, the Q♦ T♦ is always preferable to the K♥ Q♦ in SF-50, and so will remain preferable in SF-80.

(4)   In SF-50, *JT* is preferable to *JTx* in the Basic Strategy but there are some exceptions identified in the Advanced Strategy. With the greater value of *JT* under SF-80, it is always preferable to *JTx*.

(5)   In the hand K♠ J♠ T♣ 9♦ 6♥, the K♠ J♠ is preferable to the inside straight with 2 high cards, K♠ J♠ T♣ 9♦, in both SF-50 and SF-80.

Similarity # 4.   When {KK, QQ,JJ}, RF3, and FL4 occur in the same hand, the preferred combination is the same in 10/7/80 as in 10/7/50.

This similarity may come as a relief to some readers. When the RF3 is *QJT*, it is even more valuable in SF-80 and is always the preferred option. When the RF3 is something other than *QJT*, the RF3 is NEVER the preferred option. The preferred combination is either {KK, QQ,JJ} or FL4 as given on line 5c of the strategy table.

Similarity # 5.   Continue to extend all single high cards into 4-card inside straights or 3-card flushes when possible. Prefer ST4i 1hi to FL3 1hi.

Although all single high cards have the potential to become straight flushes, there is only a 1 in 178,365 chance of this when the high card is an A or K, a 2 in 178,365 chance when it is a Q, and 3 in 178,365 chance when it is a J. Even when the high card is a J, the $EV is increased by only a quarter of a cent when the payout on the straight flush is increased to 80. It happens that these increases are too small to influence the principle that single high cards should be extended into 4-card inside straights or 3-card flushes when possible.

7.4. Differences between SF-50 and SF-80 Basic Strategy

The only times when there are differences in Basic Strategy between SF-50 and SF-80 are when one of the hand alternatives is a 4-card or 3-card straight flush. In the Advanced Strategy, we will see that there are also some conditions in which there are differences when one of the hand alternatives is a 2-card royal flush or even a 2-card straight flush.

The arrangement of the SF-80 Basic Strategy table is such that the line numbers tie in wherever possible with those for SF-50. This is designed to make cross comparisons easier. Line numbers quoted below refer to both strategy tables unless otherwise specified.

It is interesting to note that there are five differences between the games at this level corresponding to SF4, SF3 +1, SF3 +0, SF3 -1, and SF3 -2.

Difference # 1: SF4

| line 2: | SF-50: | ST5 > SF4 any |
| | SF-80: | ST5 > SF4 any (except *QJT9, JT98* > ST5) |

In SF-50 as well as all games of Jacks or Better, a paying straight is always preferable to a 4-card straight flush. The two most powerful SF4s are **QJT9** and **JT98**. When part of a paying straight in SF-80, **QJT9** has a $EV of $25.53, while **JT98** has a $EV of $25.22. This is greater than the $25 from holding the straight. There are no other SF4s that are worth more than a paying straight when in the same hand as the straight. Although all 4-card open-ended straight flushes with no high cards are worth $25.43 when unpenalized, this drops to $24.89 when the fifth card to the straight is present. A SF4 must be both open-ended and contain at least one high card in order to be preferable to a paying straight.

Difference # 2: SF3 +1

line 7:   SF-50:   low pair [22 – 44] > SF3 +1[**JT9**, **QJ9**] > low pair [55 – TT]

SF-80:   SF3 +1 [**JT9**, **QJ9**] > low pair [22 – TT]

One of the easier aspects of SF-50 strategy to remember is that the best 3-card straight flushes, **JT9** and **QJ9**, are worth more than the lesser-valued low pairs, 55 – TT. When the straight flush pays 80 rather than 50, the increase in value of **JT9** and **QJ9** makes them more valuable than all low pairs, including 22 – 44.

Difference # 3: SF3 +0

lines 8 & 9:   SF-50:   AKQJ > SF3 +0 > AHHT, KQJ9

SF-80:   SF3 +0 > AKQJ (except **KH9** < AKQJ) > AHHT, KQJ9

In SF-50, SF3 +0 is preferable to a 4-card inside straight with three high cards (AHHT, KQJ9) or any combination of unsuited high cards. In SF-80, it is superior by a larger amount. When in the same hand as AKQJ, the only SF3 +0 that are possible are **KQ9**, **KJ9**, and **QJ8**. It is only the last one of these, **QJ8**, that is more valuable than AKQJ. This is the only one of the three where there is no interference with its straight potential. Although it makes no difference to strategy, this part of the rule could also have been written as:

SF-80:   AKQJ > SF3 +0 (except AKQJ < **QJ8**)

The reason for writing it the first way is that the positive extra value from always holding **QJ8** rather than always holding AKQJ is more than the combined extra value from holding AKQJ rather than **KQ9** or **KJ9**. If you were to forget the complete rule and could not work it out or look it up, you would be better off always holding SF3 +0 rather than always holding AKQJ.

Difference # 4: SF3 -1

lines 10-14:   SF-50:   **QJ**, **KH** > SF3 -1 > **AH**

SF-80:   SF3 -1 > **QJ**, **KH**, **AH**

94

We have discussed previously how the most valuable combination of two suited high cards is *QJ*, followed by *KH*, and then finally by *AH*. In SF-50, a SF3 -1 is normally only preferable to the least valuable, *AH*. In SF-80 Basic Strategy, SF3 -1 is preferable to all *HH* combinations, although we will see in the Advanced Strategy that there is a single exception.

Difference # 5: SF3 -2

    lines 15-18:   SF-50:   ST4i 1hi > QJT > QJ, *QT*, *JT* > SF3 -2

                         SF-80:   SF3 -2 > ST4i 1hi > QJT > QJ, *QT*, *JT*

Whereas SF3 -2 is always less valuable than QJT in SF-50, it is always more valuable in SF-80. In both games, QJT is always more valuable than QJ, *QT*, or *JT*. There is also a presumption (albeit with a significant exception in Level 4) that SF3 -2 is preferable to ST4i 1hi.

Lurking behind this relationship in SF-80 are some very peculiar situations. The first one of these comes from the fact that, if you compare the hands T♣ J♣ Q♥ 6♦ 3♠ and T♣ J♣ 4♥ 6♦ 3♠, the T♣ J♣ Q♥ in the first hand has less value than the T♣ J♣ in the second hand. Even though we say that QJT should always be preferred to {QJ, *QT*, *JT*}, you are better off if you are dealt T♣ J♣ unaccompanied by the Q♥. This does not mean that you should prefer T♣ J♣ to T♣ J♣ Q♥. The Q♥ is a powerful penalty to the T♣ J♣ that significantly reduces its value. QJT is always preferable to {QJ, *QT*, *JT*}.

A second major problem with this relationship is that, outside of penalty card situations, the combination that has the highest value is actually the *JT*. So why have we put it at the end rather than the beginning of the list? The reason is that these combinations create an impenetrable circle or "black hole" owing to the ways in which penalty cards work on the various combinations.

There is no question that SF3 -2 is preferable to QJT in SF-80. The only SF3 -2 that is possible in the presence of QJT without creating a higher-ranking 4-card open-ended or inside straight with two high cards is *T76*. This is worth half a cent more that QJT. There is also no question that, when *QT* or *JT* are in the same hand as QJ, the preferred combination is QJT. The problem is that, as a general presumption, *JT* is more valuable than SF3 -2. We have gone full circle with *JT* > SF3 -2 > QJT > *JT*.

In the SF-80 Basic Strategy table, we are placing *JT* below SF3 -2 and QJT for two reasons. First, *JT* is likely to occur in combination with QJT far more often than it is with SF3 -2. Second, it is easy to remember {QJ, *QT*, *JT*} as a trio of hand options of similar rank. In the Advanced Strategy table, all the penalty card considerations regarding these combinations are identified and, when followed correctly, give rise to no errors.

7.5. Basic Strategy Examples for 10/7/80 Double Bonus

This is a random set of examples designed to demonstrate the above differences in strategy (as well as some of the similarities) between SF-50 and SF-80. It is followed by a practice session that is designed to see how well you can do on your own. When the hand includes a paying combination, it is indicated in parentheses.

1.　7♣ Q♥ J♠ T♣ 6♣. It is easy to recognize Q♥ J♠ T♣ in this hand, which is always more valuable than {QJ, *QT*, *JT*} in both SF-50 and SF-80. However, it is easy either to miss the SF3 -2, 7♣ T♣ 6♣, or to assume that this worst of all SF3s cannot be worth holding in the face of the Q♥ J♠ T♣. After all, we know that {QJ, *QT*, *JT*} is preferable to SF3 -2 in 10/7/50, and, if we remember back to games of Jacks or Better, SF3 -2 is only held if there is absolutely nothing else worth holding. Things change when the straight flush pays 80; SF3 -2 rises above QJT. Prefer 7♣ T♣ 6♣ to Q♥ T♣ J♠

2.　Q♣ 9♣ 4♠ 4♦ J♣. In SF-50, SF3 +1 is more valuable than the set of lesser-valued low pairs, 55 – TT, but less valuable than the set of higher-valued low pairs, 22 – 44. In SF-80, Difference # 2 indicates that SF3 +1 is preferable to all low pairs, including those that have the potential to become bonus quads, 2s – 4s. Prefer Q♣ 9♣ J♣ to 4♠ 4♦.

3.　9♥ T♥ Q♣ 8♥ J♥ (straight). In SF-50 as well as in all games of Jacks or Better, there is no exception to the principle that a paying straight should only be broken for a 4-card royal flush. In SF-80, however, we have Difference # 1, which says that a paying straight should be broken for *QJT9* or *JT98*. Break 9♥ T♥ Q♣ 8♥ J♥ and hold 9♥ T♥ 8♥ J♥.

4.　K♥ A♥ 3♥ T♦ 9♦. The question in this hand is whether the K♥ A♥ should or should not be extended into the FL3 1hi, K♥ A♥ 3♥. Since neither of the alternatives has the possibility of becoming a straight flush, the answer is the same in both SF-50 and SF-80. Always extend *AH* into *AHx* when possible. Hold K♥ A♥ 3♥.

5.　T♥ 9♦ Q♣ 9♥ J♥. There are three options in this hand: the low pair, 9♦ 9♥; the SF3 +1, T♥ 9♥ J♥; and the open-ended straight, T♥ 9♦ Q♣ J♥ (or T♥ Q♣ 9♥ J♥). We know from SF-50 that T♥ 9♥ J♥ is preferable to 9♦ 9♥, but does its higher value under SF-80 make it preferable to the open-ended straight? The answer is NO. Prefer T♥ 9♦ Q♣ J♥ (or T♥ Q♣ 9♥ J♥) to T♥ 9♥ J♥ as per lines 6 and 7 of the strategy table.

6.　J♥ T♥ Q♦ 4♥ Q♥ (pair jacks or better). We appreciate that some players love to hate hands in which all three combinations, {KK, QQ, JJ}, RF3, and FL4, are present. This, however, is an easy one. In both SF-50 and SF-80, whenever *QJT* is present in a hand that also includes {KK, QQ, JJ} and FL4, it is ALWAYS the preferred combination. Prefer J♥ T♥ Q♥ to both Q♦ Q♥ and J♥ T♥ 4♥ Q♥.

7.   J♣ K♦ A♠ 5♣ 7♦. When there are three high cards of different suits of which one is an ace, General Principle # 7 (a) says to drop the ace. This is unaffected by whether the game is SF-50 or SF-80. Prefer J♣ K♦ to J♣ K♦ A♠.

8.   K♣ A♦ Q♠ J♣ 9♣. Although there is a general presumption in SF-80 that SF3 +0 is preferable to AKQJ, there is an important exception that is identified in the Basic Strategy table. Line 8 says, "SF3 +0 > AKQJ (except *KH9* < AKQJ)." Whenever *KH9* is present in the same hand as AKQJ, there is inevitably a straight penalty. In this hand, K♣ J♣ 9♣ is penalized by the Q♠. Prefer K♣ A♦ Q♠ J♣ to K♣ J♣ 9♣.

9.   4♦ J♥ 9♣ 8♦ 7♦. We know from Principle # 11 (a) that a single high card should be extended into 4-card inside straight when possible. This holds true in SF-50 and SF-80. J♥ 9♣ 8♦ 7♦ is therefore preferable to the J♥ alone. Harder to spot in this hand is the SF3 -2, 4♦ 8♦ 7♦. Difference # 5 instructs us that ST4i 1hi is of more value than SF3 -2 in SF-50, but of less value in SF-80. We will find in Level 4 that there is an important exception to this. Correct Basic Strategy is to prefer 4♦ 8♦ 7♦ to J♥ 9♣ 8♦ 7♦.

10.   K♠ 6♠ T♠ J♠ J♥ (pair jacks or better). This is another hand that includes all three combinations, {KK, QQ, JJ}, RF3, and FL4. The strategies in SF-50 and SF-80 are without exception identical when all three all present. The footnote to all Level 3 and 4 strategy tables tells us that, if the RF3 is other than *QJT*, the choice is between {KK, QQ, JJ} and FL4 as given in line 5c of the tables. Because the full house pays 10 in 10/7/80, a FL4 must have three high cards to be preferable to {KK, QQ, JJ}. Since K♠ 6♠ T♠ J♠ only contains two high cards, hold the high pair, J♠ J♥.

11.   6♣ T♥ 7♥ 9♥ 8♥ (straight). Should you hold the paying straight or break it for the open-ended SF4, T♥ 7♥ 9♥ 8♥? It is interesting to note that an open-ended SF4 has a $EV of more than $25 when it is not penalized. However, the 6p reduces this to below $25 and the preferred play is to hold the paying straight. You only break a straight in 10/7/80 for an open-ended SF4 that has one or two high cards.

12.   Q♥ A♦ 9♦ T♥ 7♦. In both SF-50 and SF-80, *QT* is always less valuable than *QTx*. However, when faced with a FL3 1hi of a different suit, there is a general presumption in SF-50, that *QT* is preferable. This hand happens to be an exception in SF-50 where the FL3 1hi is preferable owing to the combined interference of the A♦ and the 9♦. In SF-80, there are no exceptions to the rule that *QT* is preferable to FL3 1hi of which it is not a part. Prefer Q♥ T♥ to A♦ 9♦ 7♦.

13.   Q♥ 4♦ 3♦ J♥ 2♦. We hope you will recognize by now that 4♦ 3♦ 2♦ is categorized as a SF3 -1 because its potential to be completed from below is restricted by its proximity to the ace. In SF-80, SF3 -1 is preferable to any two suited high cards apart from one exception identified in the Advanced Strategy. Prefer 4♦ 3♦ 2♦ to Q♥ J♥.

14.   T♣ 8♣ J♣ 6♣ 9♣ (flush). This hand is a paying flush that contains the powerful 4-card straight flush, T♣ 8♣ J♣ 9♣. Although it is appropriate to break a paying

straight for *JT98* as provided in Difference # 1, it is only ever appropriate to break a paying flush for a 4-card royal flush. Hold all five cards.

15. K♣ Q♣ J♥ 9♥ 8♥. In SF-50, a SF3 +0 is superior to any two suited high cards or to an inside straight with three high cards. In SF-80, it is preferable by an even larger margin. Prefer J♥ 9♥ 8♥ to K♣ Q♣ J♥ 9♥ or K♣ Q♣.

16. A♣ K♦ K♣ A♥ T♣ (two pair). The alternatives in this hand are: the 3-card royal flush, A♣ K♣ T♣; the two pair, A♣ K♦ K♣ A♥; and the pair of aces, A♣ A♥. Since none of these combinations has the potential to become a straight flush, the preferred combination is the same in SF-50 and SF-80. We know that two pair is always preferable to a 3-card royal. The question then boils down to whether we should break the two pair and go for the aces. We know from SF-50 strategy that we should break the two pair in 9/7 but not in 10/7. Since the full house always pays 10 when the straight flush pays 80, it is better to keep the two pair. Prefer A♣ K♦ K♣ A♥ to A♣ A♥.

17. 6♣ T♦ Q♦ 9♣ 5♣. The choice in this hand is between the Q♦ T♦ and the SF3 -2, 6♣ 9♣ 5♣. In SF-50, *QT* is always preferable to SF3 -2. In SF-80, the situation is reversed with SF3 -2 always preferable to *QT*. Prefer 6♣ 9♣ 5♣ to T♦ Q♦.

18. Q♥ A♦ J♥ K♦ 8♥. Although AKQJ is always preferable to SF3 +0 in SF-50, Difference # 3 tells us that AKQJ has less value than *QJ8* in SF-80. The possibility that Q♥ J♥ 8♥ may become a completed straight, flush, or straight flush is not penalized by any other card in the hand. Prefer Q♥ J♥ 8♥ to Q♥ A♦ J♥ K♦.

19. 3♦ K♣ A♦ Q♣ 5♦. It is easy to recognize in this hand that the two suited high cards, K♣ Q♣, are preferable to the three high cards of mixed suits, K♣ A♦ Q♣. The combination that is harder to recognize is the 3-card straight flush, 3♦ A♦ 5♦. All 3-card straight flushes that include an ace are double inside with a single high card, and are therefore categorized as SF3 -1. Although SF3 -1 is generally less valuable than *KH* in SF-50, it is always more valuable in SF-80. Prefer 3♦ A♦ 5♦ to K♣ Q♣.

20. 9♦ 8♦ 5♦ J♥ T♥. This looks like a straightforward comparison between the SF3 -2, 9♦ 8♦ 5♦, and the J♥ T♥. When the straight flush pays 80, SF3 -2 rises above *JT*. The 9♦ 8♦ 5♦ has more value than J♥ T♥, but it is not the preferred combination. Whenever you are comparing two alternative combinations, always make sure that you are not missing a third. This hand also contains the open-ended straight, 9♦ 8♦ J♥ T♥, which has significantly more value that either 9♦ 8♦ 5♦ or J♥ T♥.

7.6. Basic Strategy Practice Session for 10/7/80 Double Bonus

The answers to these questions do not necessarily apply to 10/7/50 or 9/7/50.

	Question						Answer				
17.	J♣	3♦	9♣	3♥	Q♣	1.		A♦	5♣	3♥	2♦
4.	Q♥	T♦	6♦	J♠	7♦	2.	T♦			J♦	9♦
20.	6♥	3♠	8♠	7♠	4♥	3.	Q♣				Q♦
11.	J♥	Q♥	8♣	9♥	T♥	4.		T♦	6♦		7♦
16.	3♦	5♦	Q♥	6♦	J♥	5.	J♥	8♥		T♥	9♥
3.	Q♣	T♣	A♣	5♣	Q♦	6.		T♥			Q♥
19.	2♣	8♦	6♦	7♦	2♠	7.	9♣	7♠		8♣	J♦
10.	J♦	A♥	T♦	Q♦	A♣	8.	T♣	K♣		J♣	5♣
1.	K♠	A♦	5♣	3♥	2♦	9.	Q♦		9♠	T♦	K♥
12.	J♥	A♣	K♥	9♥	Q♠	10.		A♥			A♣
6.	7♠	T♥	K♠	5♠	Q♥	11.	J♥	Q♥		9♥	T♥
18.	J♣	7♣	Q♣	8♠	9♠	12.	J♥	A♣	K♥		Q♠
15.	8♦	A♣	3♣	2♦	5♣	13.	K♦	T♥	J♦	9♦	Q♦
2.	T♦	4♣	4♠	J♦	9♦	14.	K♦		J♦		Q♦
8.	T♣	K♣	A♦	J♣	5♣	15.		A♣	3♣		5♣
5.	J♥	8♥	Q♣	T♥	9♥	16.	3♦	5♦		6♦	
13.	K♦	T♥	J♦	9♦	Q♦	17.	J♣		9♣		Q♣
7.	9♣	7♠	5♥	8♣	J♦	18.	J♣		Q♣		
14.	K♦	5♠	J♦	J♥	Q♦	19.	2♣				2♠
9.	Q♦	7♠	9♠	T♦	K♥	20.	6♥ 3♠ 7♠ 4♥ or 6♥ 8♠ 7♠ 4♥				

Chapter 8

Level 4: "Advanced Strategy" for 10/7/80 Double Bonus

8.1. Advanced Strategy Table for 10/7/80

Select the hand option that appears highest in the following list:

1: RF5; SF5; 4-OF-A-KIND

2: RF4 > FL5, ST5 > SF4 (except *QJT9*, *JT98* > ST5)

3: AAA > FULL HOUSE > 3-OF-A-KIND others

4: TWO PAIR > AA

5a* *QJT* > FL4 all > RF3 others   (*KQJx* < *KQJ* with neither sp nor high pair also present)

5b* *KQJ*, *QJT* > KK, QQ, JJ > RF3 others   (KK, QQ, JJ < *KHT* with neither fp nor sp)

5c* FL4 3hi > KK, QQ, JJ > FL4 others

6: ST4 non-inside [2345 – KQJT]

7: SF3 +1 [*JT9*, *QJ9*] > low pair [22 – TT]

          ([55 – TT] < SF3 +0 containing no high card, with neither hsp nor low-pair sp)

8: SF3 +0 > AKQJ (except *KH9* < AKQJ)

9: AHHT, KQJ9

10: SF3 -1 ([A-low] < *QJ*)

11: *QJ*

12: FL3 2 hi (< *KH* with no sp)

13: *KH*

14: *AH*

15: KQJ;

16: ST4i 2hi > SF3 -2 > ST4i 1hi   (SF3 -2 with sp < ST4i 1hi)

                                     (SF3 -2 < *JT* with neither 8p nor 9p)

                                       (JT87 < *JT* with neither fp nor hsp)

                                       (from *JT* "874" or *JT* "975", prefer SF3 -2 to ST4i 1hi or *JT*)

17: QJT > QJ, *JT*

18: FL3 1hi [*QTx*] > *QT* > FL3 1hi [others]   (FL3 1hi < KH with no sp)

19: KH (< AKH when 9p)

20: A (< AH when both fp and lsp, except when Tp unsuited with A) (< *KT* with no 9p and when sfp to A)

21: *KT*

22: K, Q, J

23: ST4i 0hi > FL3 0hi

24: five new cards (< SF2 [*45*, *89*, *9T*] with no sp other than a single sp at the extreme)**

* Lines 5a, 5b, and 5c cover those situations in which a hand contains any two of the three combinations: {KK, QQ, JJ}, FL4, and RF3. If all three are present, use the following rule:
     "If the RF3 is *QJT*, hold *QJT*. If the RF3 is other than *QJT*, the preferred combination is either {KK, QQ, JJ} or FL4, and can be determined from line 5c alone."

** This is a slight simplification. See the appendix for the precise conditions.

8.2. Exceptions to Basic Strategy Table for 10/7/80

The main references to hand options are identical in both the Advanced Strategy table and the Basic Strategy table with the same line numbers. The Advanced Strategy table differs from the Basic by the inclusion of secondary references contained in parentheses in which there is an exception to the Basic Strategy rankings caused by penalty cards.

Exception # 1 line 5a:

> *KQJx* (< *KQJ* with neither sp nor high pair also present)

In SF-50, *QJT* is the only RF3 that is more valuable than FL4. In SF-80, K-high 3-card royals have more value than in SF-50 owing to their straight flush potential. RF3 [K-high] may be of the form *KQJ* or *KHT*. However, it is only with *KQJ* where there is a condition in which it becomes more valuable than FL4. The *KQJ* must be free of any penalty (other than the fourth card to the flush) for it to be more valuable than *KQJx*. Not only must it free of any straight penalty, which could be A, T, or 9, it must also be free of any high pair penalty, which could be K, Q, or J.

For example, from the hand K♥ Q♥ J♥ 8♦ 5♥, hold K♥ Q♥ J♥ 5♥ in SF-50, but hold K♥ Q♥ J♥ in SF-80 because it is not penalized by the remaining card. If the 8♦ had been a straight penalty or a high-pair penalty in the form of an A, K, Q, J, T, or 9, the preferred play would have been K♥ Q♥ J♥ 5♥ in SF-80 as well as SF-50.

Exception # 2 line 5b: KK, QQ, JJ (< *KHT* with neither fp nor sp)

The two most valuable 3-card royals are *QJT* and *KQJ*. They both have two more high cards than insides and are both ALWAYS more valuable than {KK, QQ, JJ}. Next in line come *AHH* and *KHT*, which both have one more high card than insides. We noted in chapter 5 that *AHH* and *KHT* have very similar $EV in SF-50. However, when the payout on the straight flush is increased from 50 to 80, the value of *KHT* is increased while the value of *AHH* remains unchanged; an A-high RF3 has no potential to become a straight flush. Provided *KHT* is not penalized either by a flush penalty or a straight penalty, it is preferable to {KK, QQ, JJ} in 10/7/80.

For example, in the hand K♣ Q♣ Q♦ T♣ 5♣, the preferred play is Q♣ Q♦ in SF-50. However, because the K♣ Q♣ T♣ is not penalized (other than by the Q♦), it is preferable to Q♣ Q♦ in SF-80.

Exception # 3 line 7:

low pair [55 – TT] (< SF3 +0 containing no high card, with neither hsp nor low-pair sp)

An important difference between SF-80 strategy and SF-50 strategy is that SF3 +1 becomes more valuable than all low pairs, including 22 – 44, which have the potential to become premium quads. In Exception # 3, we see that there is also an extreme condition in which SF3 +0 can be more valuable than the lower-valued pairs, 55 – TT. We use the word extreme because this is a very restrictive condition.

This condition refers only to SF3 +0 that contain no high cards. The possibility that SF3 +0 will turn into a completed straight flush is higher the fewer the number of insides. For example, *678* may become *45678*, *56789*, and *6789T*. However, *89J* may become *789TJ* and *89TJQ*, while *8JQ* can only become *89TJQ*. The higher payout on the straight flush has triple the impact on the $EV of *678* than it does on *8JQ*. It is only a SF3 +0 that contains no high cards and no insides that gains in value sufficiently from the higher paying straight flush such that it is ever preferable to a low pair. (Although *QJ9* and *JT9* both contain high cards, they come under the category of SF3 +1 and are always more valuable than low pair [55 – TT] in both SF-50 and SF-80.)

When SF3 +0 has no insides, the only relevant straight penalty is one at the extreme. An adjacent straight penalty would create a higher-ranking 4-card open-ended straight. The impact of a straight penalty at the extreme is greater when it is a high card. As well as penalizing the potential for a straight, a "high straight penalty" penalizes the potential for the combination to end up "merely" as a high pair. To be eligible in this condition, the SF3 +0 can only have a non-high-card straight penalty that is at the extreme.

A final requirement in the above condition is that the low pair cannot itself be a pair of straight penalties to the SF3 +0. To make this a clearer, here are some examples:

from	hold	why
5♣ 5♦ 8♠ 9♠ T♠	8♠ 9♠ T♠	8♠ 9♠ T♠ is unpenalized and contains no high card
3♥ 4♥ 5♥ 5♣ 7♣	3♥ 4♥ 5♥	3♥ 4♥ 5♥ only has a single sp at the extreme, the 7♣
9♥ T♥ Q♥ 7♣ 7♠	7♣ 7♠	9♥ T♥ Q♥ is not eligible since it contains a high card
5♣ 6♣ 7♣ 9♦ 9♥	9♦ 9♥	9♦ 9♥ represents a pair of sp to the 5♣ 6♣ 7♣
8♦ 9♦ T♦ T♣ Q♠	T♦ T♣	8♦ 9♦ T♦ has a high-card straight penalty, the Q♠
4♣ 4♦ 5♦ 6♦ T♣	4♣ 4♦	only low pairs [55 – TT] are ever < SF3 +0
2♣ 3♣ 4♣ 7♦ 7♠	7♦ 7♠	2♣ 3♣ 4♣ is a SF3 -1, not a SF3 +0

Exception # 4 line 10:　　　　SF3 -1 [A-low] < *QJ*

On first examination, this condition looks wrong. The ace in the SF3 -1 penalizes the *QJ* but the *QJ* does not penalize the ability of SF3 [A-low] to become a straight. With the penalty conditions weighing on the *QJ* and not the SF3 -1, how can it be that this can give rise to the exception in which *QJ* is preferable? If "SF3 -1 [A-low] < *QJ*," why then is not "SF3 -1 [2-low] < *QJ*" since the *QJ* would be free of any interference.

The answer is that this is not caused by penalty cards. In SF-80, trading off an inside for a high card in the SF3 classification system is much less even than in SF-50. One less inside brings more value than an additional high card. For example,

$EV of **A23** increases from $2.84 to $2.97 from SF-50 to SF-80

$EV of **234** increases from $2.88 to $3.16 from SF-50 to SF-80

The value of **A23** (with one high card and two insides) is increased by 13¢ while the value of **234** (with no high cards and only one inside) is increased by 28¢.

SF3 [A-low] is the only SF3 -1 that contains a high card that can be present with **QJ** without creating a higher-ranking 4-card straight.

In chapter 6: Exception # 3 (c), we made special note of the hand **AJ**"Q98". As well as containing the **AJ** and the SF3 -1, **Q98**, this hand also contains the ST4i 2hi, JQ98. In SF-80, there is no situation where SF3 -1 is inferior to ST4i 2hi, and only the single case in Exception # 4 above where SF3 -1 is inferior to two suited high cards. In the hand A♣ Q♦ J♣ 9♦ 8♦, hold A♣ J♣ in SF-50, but hold Q♦ 9♦ 8♦ in SF-80.

Exception # 5 line 12:   FL3 2hi (< **KH** with no sp)

This condition is identical in SF-50 and SF-80. It was covered in Exception # 1 in chapter 6.

Exception # 6 (a) line 16:   SF3 -2 (< ST4i 1hi when sp)

This is one of the easier penalty card situations in 10/7/80. Any SF3 -2 with a straight penalty is inferior to a 4-card inside straight with one high card. For example, the hand Q♣ T♥ 9♦ 8♦ 5♦ contains the SF3 -2, 9♦ 8♦ 5♦, and the ST4i 1hi, Q♣ T♥ 9♦ 8♦. Since 9♦ 8♦ 5♦ is unpenalized, it is preferable to Q♣ T♥ 9♦ 8♦. In contrast, in the hand Q♣ T♦ 9♦ 8♥ 6♦, the T♦ 9♦ 6♦ is penalized by the 8♥ and is inferior to Q♣ T♦ 9♦ 8♥.

When a hand contains an ace and a cluster of very low cards, always be on the lookout for an A-low 4-card straight and remember that all A-low 4-card straights must be deemed to have an inside. For example, in the hand A♥ 2♥ 3♣ 4♣ 7♣, prefer the unpenalized 3♣ 4♣ 7♣ to A♥ 2♥ 3♣ 4♣. However, in the hand A♥ 2♣ 3♣ 4♣ 6♣, prefer A♥ 2♣ 3♣ 4♣ to the penalized 2♣ 3♣ 6♣.

Exception # 6 (b) line 16:   SF3 -2 (< **JT** with neither 8p nor 9p)

In SF-50, **JT** is always preferable to SF3 -2. In SF-80, the values of both **JT** and SF3 -2 are increased, but the increase is much greater for SF3 -2 than for **JT**. A combination that begins with three cards to a straight flush has a much larger proportion of its $EV arising from the possibility of becoming a completed straight flush than does a combination that begins with only two cards to a straight flush. Provided there is no 8p or 9p, *JT* is preferable to SF3 -2 in SF-80. It is okay if there is a single 7p to the *JT*.

For example: in the hand J♥ T♥ 7♣ 6♣ 3♣,   prefer J♥ T♥ to 7♣ 6♣ 3♣

                  in the hand J♥ T♥ 8♣ 6♣ 4♣,   prefer 8♣ 6♣ 4♣ to J♥ T♥

It is possible for *JT* and SF3 -2 to occur in the same hand as a ST4i 1hi. We will see in Exception # 6 (d) that the SF3 -2 is always preferable in these situations.

Exception # 6 (c) line 16:   ST4i 1hi [JT87] (< *JT* with neither fp nor hsp)

In SF-50, it is always beneficial to extend *JT* into ST4i 1hi when possible in the form of JT97 or JT87. In SF-80, *JT* has more value than in SF-50 owing to its potential to become a straight flush. This increase is sufficient to make *JT* more valuable than JT87 provided the fifth card does not penalize the *JT* by being a flush penalty or a high-card straight penalty in the form of an A or K. (Note that if the fifth card is a Q, the hand also contains a higher-ranking ST4i 2 hi). *JT* is never preferable to JT97 because 9p+7p is a more powerful combination of straight penalties than 8p+7p. See Exception # 6 (d) for situations in which these hand combinations are also accompanied by a SF3 -2.

Exception # 6 (d) line 16:

        from *JT* "874" or *JT* "975", prefer SF3 -2 to ST4i 1hi or *JT*

This is really a clarification rather than an exception. It is possible for SF3 -2, ST4i 1hi, and *JT* to occur in the same hand in the form of *JT* "874" or *JT* "975". In both cases, the SF3 -2 has no straight penalty while the *JT* is penalized by an 8 or 9. In both cases, hold the SF3 -2.

Exception # 7 line 18:   FL3 1hi (< KH with no sp)

This condition is identical in SF-50 and SF-80. It was covered in chapter 6 in Exception # 1 (b).

Exception # 8 line 19:   KH (< AKQ, AKJ when 9p)

Again, this condition is identical in SF-50 and SF-80. It was covered in chapter 6 in Exception # 6.

Exception # 9 line 20:

        A (< AH when both fp and lsp, except when Tp unsuited with A)

        A (< *KT* with no 9p when sfp to A)

Even though an ace alone has greater value in SF-80 than SF-50, the very restrictive penalty card situation in which an ace alone has less value than AH is identical in the two games. This was discussed at length in chapter 6. In SF-80, there is also a condition in which an ace is less valuable than *KT*. Although this is presented in a separate set of parentheses, it could be considered as an exception to the condition included in the first set of parentheses. Here are some examples:

In the hand A♣ K♦ T♦ 6♣ 3♠, the A♣ is faced with both the flush penalty, the 6♣, and the low straight penalty, the 3♠. Together, these penalties are sufficient to make the A♣ K♦ preferable to the ace alone, except when there is a Tp unsuited with the ace. Since this hand contains the T♦, holding the A♣ is preferable to the A♣ K♦ despite its flush penalty and low straight penalty. Frequent players of SF-50 soon learn to hold the ace alone when accompanied by *KT*.

In SF-80, the value of *KT* is raised sufficiently such that there is an "exception to the exception" regarding a T that is unsuited with the ace. The second condition above says that an ace has less value than *KT* when there is no 9p to the *KT* and when there is a straight flush penalty to the ace. The absence of a 9p means that the *KT* must be without penalty (except for the ace). A 9p is the only one that can interfere with *KT* (if a Q or a J were present, the hand would contain the much higher-ranking AHHT). A straight flush penalty is more damaging to an ace than a straight penalty plus a flush penalty because, as well as penalizing the prospects of a straight and a flush, it eliminates the possibility of a straight flush.

The hand A♥ K♠ T♣ 8♣ 5♥ is played differently in SF-50 and SF-80. In SF-50, the A♥ is preferred to the A♥ K♠ because the A♥ is "rescued" by the unsuited T♦, even though it is penalized by the 5♥, which is both a flush penalty and a low straight penalty. However, in SF-80, the K♠ T♣ is the preferred play because it has no 9p while the 5♥ is a powerful straight flush penalty to the A♥.

Exception # 10 line 24:

five new cards < SF2 [*45*, *89*, *9T*] with no sp other than a single sp at the extreme

When the payout on the straight flush is raised to 80, the values of 2-card straight flushes are raised such that there are conditions in which a 2-card straight flush can be preferable to drawing five new cards. The rule presented above is a simplification. The precise rules are presented in the appendix.

When a SF2 is consecutive and free of any penalty, it is always preferable to five new cards. However, it is not common to find this in the absence of a higher-ranking combination such as a single high card, a 4-card inside straight, or a 3-card flush. If the SF2 has a straight penalty that is not at the extreme, or two straight penalties at the extreme, it is never preferable to five new cards. Even when there is a single straight penalty at the extreme, there are instances that are covered in the appendix in which five new cards may still be preferable depending upon the ranks and suits of the remaining cards.

The reason why the rule above is limited to SF2 [*45, 89, 9T*] is that it is not possible for SF2 [*56, 67, 78*] to have only a single straight penalty at the extreme without a high card or low pair also being present. For example, the two straight penalties at the extreme to *56* are 2 and 9. If only one of these is present, it is necessary for the remaining two cards to be outside the range of 2 to 9. This is not possible without one of them being a high card or both of them being a low pair. Here are some examples:

from	hold	why
9♣ T♣ 2♦ 3♣ 4♥	9♣ T♣	9♣ T♣ is not penalized in any way
8♥ 9♥ 5♦ 4♣ 3♠	8♥ 9♥	there is only a single sp at the extreme to 8♥ 9♥
4♠ 5♠ 7♦ 9♣ T♣	nothing	the 7♦ is a sp NOT at the extreme to 4♠ 5♠ and 9♣ T♣
8♥ 9♥ 4♦ 3♣ 2♥	8♥ 9♥ 2♥	always prefer FL3 to SF2
4♦ 5♦ 7♣ 8♣ T♠	4♦ 5♦ 7♣ 8♣	prefer ST4i 0hi [4♦ 5♦ 7♣ 8♣] to either 4♦ 5♦ or 7♣ 8♣
5♦ 6♦ 9♣ T♥ 2♥	nothing	5♦ 6♦ has two sp at the extreme, the 9♣ and 2♥; Five new cards are always > SF2 [*56, 67,* or *78*]

8.3. Some important differences between SF-50 and SF-80 Advanced Strategy.

The list of exceptions above included some without discussion where the penalty card conditions are identical in SF-50 and SF-80. However, those of you who are familiar with the SF-50 Advanced Strategy may be interested in the penalty card conditions in SF-50 that do not apply in SF-80. Although some of these are implicit in the differences between SF-50 and SF-80 Basic Strategies, they are worthy of identifying explicitly. These are conditions in which combinations that have the potential to form a straight flush are neck and neck with combinations that have either much less or no potential to form a straight flush.

(1)   In SF-50, there are penalty card conditions in which SF3 -1 is of less value than *KH*, *AH*, and ST4i 2hi. In SF-80, SF3 -1 is always more valuable than these combinations.

(2)   In SF-50, there are conditions under which SF3 -2 is of less value *QT*, or a single high card in the form of an A or J. There are no such exceptions in SF-80.

(3)   In SF-50, there are exceptions to the basic presumption that both *JT* and *QT* are preferable to a FL3 1hi of a different suit. In SF-80, both *JT* and *QT* are increased in value by their potential to form straight flushes, while FL3 1hi is unchanged in value. In SF-80, *JT* and *QT* are always preferable to a FL3 1hi of which they are not a part.

8.4. Advanced Strategy Examples for 10/7/80

1.   K♦ A♣ 6♠ T♦ 3♣. In SF-50, the A♣ alone has more value in this hand than the K♦ A♣. Although the 3♣ represents both a flush penalty and a low straight penalty to the A♣, the T♦ is a Tp that is unsuited with the ace and "rescues" the ace. Holding the K♦ T♦ is never a consideration. However, in SF-80, Exception # 9 identifies a condition in which *KT* is preferable to an ace. The *KT* must be free of interference (except from the ace), while the ace must have a straight flush penalty. These conditions exist in this hand. Prefer K♦ T♦ to A♣.

2.   4♦ 3♣ 7♣ 7♥ 5♦. It would be easy simply to hold 7♣ 7♥ in this hand without noticing the possibility of the SF3 +0, 4♦ 3♦ 5♦. Although it would represent poor technique not to have considered 4♦ 3♦ 5♦, it is correct to hold 7♣ 7♥ they represent a pair of straight penalties to 4♦ 3♦ 5♦.

3.   4♣ 8♥ T♠ 5♣ 9♦. The only combination worth considering in this hand is the SF2, 4♣ 5♣. Since it is only penalized by the 8♥, which is a straight penalty at the extreme, hold 4♣ 5♣ rather than drawing five new cards as per Exception # 10.

4.   7♣ T♥ J♥ 4♠ 8♦. When a hand contains only a single high card or a high card with suited T, always check whether it can be extended into a 4-card inside straight. In this hand, the T♥ J♥ can be extended into 7♣ T♥ J♥ 8♦. In SF-50, an inside straight with one high card is ALWAYS preferable to a single high card or high card with suited T. However, SF-80 contains Exception # 6 (c), which tells us that JT87 is less valuable than *JT* provided there is no flush penalty or high-card straight penalty to *JT*. In this hand, T♥ J♥ is free of these penalties and is preferable to 7♣ T♥ J♥ 8♦.

5.   J♥ K♥ 5♣ Q♥ 2♥. The alternatives in this hand are the 3-card royal flush, J♥ K♥ Q♥, and the 4-card flush, J♥ K♥ Q♥ 2♥. In SF-50, the only RF3 that is ever preferable (and is always preferable) to FL4 is *QJT*. Every other RF3 has less value than FL4. However, in SF-80, *KQJ* is more valuable than *KQJx* provided it is not penalized in any way other than by the fourth card to the flush. Since the 5♣ does not penalize the J♥ K♥ Q♥, the correct play in SF-80 is to hold J♥ K♥ Q♥ rather than J♥ K♥ Q♥ 2♥.

6.   4♥ 6♥ 7♦ 8♥ A♣. In both SF-50 and SF-80, a 4-card inside straight with no high cards is only preferable to a 3-card flush with no high cards. It is always inferior to any high card or 3-card straight flush. Since this hand contains both the A♣ and the SF3 -2, 4♥ 6♥ 8♥, we may forget about 4♥ 6♥ 7♦ 8♥. Long time players of SF-50 Advanced Strategy will no doubt have committed to memory the rule that SF3 -2 with a straight penalty is less valuable than a solitary ace. This hand satisfies that condition. However, although there are several penalty card conditions that remain unchanged in SF-80, this is not one of them. All SF3s have greater value in SF-80, and there is no condition in which SF3 -2 is less valuable than a single high card. Prefer the 4♥ 6♥ 8♥ to the A♣.

7.   6♥ J♣ 8♥ T♣ 4♥. In SF-50, *JT* is always more valuable than SF3 -2. However, Exception # 6 (b) tells us it has less value in SF-80 when *JT* is penalized by a 9 or an 8. In this hand, J♣ T♣ is penalized by the 8♥, so prefer 6♥ 8♥ 4♥ to J♣ T♣.

8.   8♣ 4♦ 7♣ 6♣ 6♥. This hand contains the SF3 +0, 8♣ 7♣ 6♣, and the low pair, 6♣ 6♥. Because the SF3 +0 has no insides, no high cards, and no high-card straight penalty, prefer 8♣ 7♣ 6♣ to 6♣ 6♥ as per Exception # 3.

9.   K♣ Q♣ J♦ T♣ J♠ (pair jacks or better). We hope you all know by now that, although KQJT is the most valuable 4-card straight, it is always inferior to a 3-card royal flush. The decision in this hand is between K♣ Q♣ T♣ and J♦ J♠. Exception # 2 states that *KHT* is more valuable than {KK, QQ, JJ} in 10/7/80 provided it has neither a straight penalty nor a flush penalty. Although there are no other cards in the hand other than the RF3 and the high pair, this does not mean that the RF3 in unpenalized. The pair of Js represent two straight penalties. Given that one straight penalty is sufficient, two are more than sufficient. Prefer J♦ J♠ to K♣ Q♣ T♣.

10.   T♥ 9♥ 2♦ 3♣ 7♠. There is nothing of value in this hand except possibly the SF2, T♥ 9♥. However, because there is a sp in the form of the 7♠, which is not at the extreme, draw five new cards.

11.   5♣ 8♦ J♦ 5♠ 9♦. Although there are some situations in which SF3 +0 has more value than a low pair [55 – TT], these only apply when the SF3 +0 contains no high cards. Prefer 5♣ 5♠ to 8♦ J♦ 9♦.

12.   J♥ A♠ K♥ Q♥ 5♥. It is easy to spot J♥ A♠ K♥ Q♥ in this hand. However, we know that any 3-card royal flush is more valuable than any type of 4-card straight. The choice here is between the 3-card royal, J♥ K♥ Q♥, and the 4-card flush, J♥ K♥ Q♥ 5♥. Exception # 1 tells us that *KQJ* is preferable to *KQJx* in 10/7/80 provided there is no straight penalty or high pair also present in the hand. Since the A♠ is a straight penalty to J♥ K♥ Q♥, prefer J♥ K♥ Q♥ 5♥ to J♥ K♥ Q♥.

13.   J♣ T♣ 3♣ 8♦ 7♥. This is a complex hand with three alternatives. As well as J♣ T♣, there is the FL3 1hi, J♣ T♣ 3♣, and the ST4i 1hi, J♣ T♣ 8♦ 7♥. Although there is a condition in SF-50 in which *JT* < *JTx*, there is no such condition in SF-80. J♣ T♣ 3♣ is not a consideration. In Exception # 6 (c), we are told that JT87 has less value than *JT* provided there is neither a flush penalty nor a high-card straight penalty to *JT*. Since the 3♣ is a flush penalty to J♣ T♣, hold J♣ T♣ 8♦ 7♥.

14.   7♦ 8♦ T♠ J♥ 4♦. This hand contains an easy-to-spot ST4i 1hi, 7♦ 8♦ T♠ J♥, and a harder-to-spot SF3 -2, 7♦ 8♦ 4♦. Since there is no straight penalty to 7♦ 8♦ 4♦, Exception # 6 (a) does not apply and 7♦ 8♦ 4♦ is preferable to 7♦ 8♦ T♠ J♥. If we could rearrange the cards into J♣ T♠ 8♦ 7♦ 4♦, it would be much easy to identify the SF3 -2 and to see that it has no straight penalty. The mark of an experienced player is not just knowing strategy by heart. It is also being able to recognize all the options contained in a hand. It would be a significant error to hold 7♦ 8♦ T♠ J♥ and miss 7♦ 8♦ 4♦.

15.   4♣ 5♣ 6♣ 9♦ 4♠. This is another example in which a low pair, 4♣ 4♠, is in competition with a SF3 +0, 4♣ 5♣ 6♣. Although there is no straight penalty to 4♣ 5♣ 6♣, it would be a mistake to hold it. It is only the lesser-valued low pairs, 55 – TT, that are ever less valuable than SF3 +0. The higher-valued low pairs, 22 – 44, are always of more value than any SF3 +0. Hold 4♣ 4♠.

16.   9♥ A♣ Q♥ J♣ 8♥. There are three main alternatives in this hand: the two suited high cards, A♣ J♣; the ST4i 2hi, 9♥ Q♥ J♣ 8♥, and the SF3 -1, 9♥ Q♥ 8♥. This particular hand was discussed specifically in chapter 6: Exception # 3 (c), where A♣ J♣ was identified as the preferred combination in SF-50. When the payout on the straight flush is increased from 50 to 80, the value of SF3 -1 is increased by a greater amount than the value of two suited high cards, while the value of an inside straight remains unchanged. In SF-80, SF3 -1 is superior to any two suited high cards except in the one situation identified in this chapter as Exception # 4 in which SF3 -1 [A-low] < *QJ*. Since this exception does not apply to this hand, prefer 9♥ Q♥ 8♥ to A♣ J♣.

17.   4♥ J♠ T♠ 7♥ 8♥. In SF-80, the relationships between SF3 -2, ST4 i 1hi, and *JT* are complex. Exceptions 6 (a), (b), and (c) deal with those situations in which any two of the three options are present in the same hand. However, this hand contains all three combinations, the 4♥ 7♥ 8♥, the J♠ T♠ 7♥ 8♥, and the J♠ T♠. Fortunately, when all three exist together, the SF3 -2 of necessity must be free of any straight penalty and is always the preferred option. Hold 4♥ 7♥ 8♥ as per Exception # 6 (d).

18.   8♠ 9♠ 2♦ 3♣ 4♠. The first combination you may notice in this hand is the SF2, 8♠ 9♠. Since it has no straight penalty, it qualifies under Exception # 10. However, one of the remaining cards is of the same suit, the 4♠. A 3-card flush is always preferable to a SF2 or five new cards, so hold 8♠ 9♠ 4♠.

19.   A♦ K♣ T♣ 5♦ 9♠. This is a relatively difficult hand. The choices are the A♦ alone, the A♦ K♣, and the K♣ T♣. The 5♦ is a straight flush penalty to the A♦. This is normally sufficient to make AH preferable to an ace alone unless the hand contains a T that is unsuited with the ace. We have such a T in this hand. However, this T is suited with the K and we know from Exception # 9 that *KT* is preferable to an ace with a straight flush penalty provided there is no straight penalty to the *KT* (other than the ace). Such a straight penalty exists in this hand in the form of the 9♠. The A♦ alone is preferable to both A♦ K♣ and K♣ T♣.

20.   J♣ 3♥ A♥ Q♣ 5♥. A General Principle of both Jacks or Better and Double Bonus is that two suited high cards are of more value than three high cards of mixed suits. J♣ Q♣ is preferable to J♣ A♥ Q♣. However, if you hold J♣ Q♣ and then review the cards you are about to discard, you will identify them as 3♥ A♥ 5♥. All A-low 3-card straight flushes are categorized as SF3 -1. Normally, SF3 -1 is preferable to any two suited high cards in SF-80. However, Exception # 4 tells us that "SF3 -1 [A-low] < *QJ*." This hand is therefore an exception to the normal rule. Hold J♣ Q♣.

8.5. Advanced Strategy Practice Session for 10/7/80

This practice session includes hands that are as difficult as any you are likely to come across in SF-80 Double Bonus. If you can get all these questions correct as well as those for SF-50, you have reached a level with few peers.

	Question							Answer				
17.	3♦	5♦	7♠	7♣	4♦		1.	K♠				T♠
4.	J♥	T♥	J♦	K♥	8♠		2.	K♥			Q♥	J♥
20.	T♥	9♥	8♥	T♣	7♦		3.	9♣		8♣	5♣	
11.	J♥	A♦	3♦	Q♥	5♦		4.	J♥	T♥	K♥		
16.	4♠	2♦	8♣	9♣	3♠		5.	K♣	K♦			
3.	9♣	T♦	8♣	5♣	Q♦		6.		7♠	7♣		
19.	J♦	6♠	T♦	7♥	8♥		7.	T♣	J♣	K♣	5♣	
10.	K♣	6♣	K♦	J♣	T♣		8.		A♦			
1.	K♠	A♦	5♦	8♥	T♠		9.		8♥	9♥		
12.	5♦	4♦	8♥	9♠	T♣		10.	K♣	K♦			
6.	8♠	J♦	7♠	7♣	9♠		11.	J♥		Q♥		
18.	5♦	J♥	Q♥	6♦	3♦		12.	5♦	4♦			
15.	5♠	4♠	T♦	9♦	2♣		13.	5♦	7♦	6♦		
2.	K♥	4♥	8♣	Q♥	J♥		14.	J♦	T♦	7♥	9♥	
8.	T♠	K♠	A♦	2♦	9♥		15.	T♦	9♦			
5.	K♣	K♦	J♣	T♣	A♦		16.	8♣	9♣			
13.	6♣	5♦	J♥	7♦	6♦		17.	7♠	7♣			
7.	T♣	J♣	K♣	5♣	9♠		18.	5♦	6♦	3♦		
14.	J♦	A♥	T♦	7♥	9♥		19.	J♦	T♦			
9.	3♦	4♦	8♥	9♥	2♣		20.	T♥ 9♥ 8♥ 7♦ or 9♥ 8♥ T♣ 7♦				

Appendix

SF2 versus Five New Cards in 10/7/80

The 10/7/80 Advanced Strategy presents the following simplified rule covering those situations in which five new cards are less valuable than SF2 [*45*, *89*, *9T*]:

"five new cards (< SF2 [*45*, *89*, *9T*] with no sp other than a single sp at the extreme)"

The precise rules are:

five new cards

> < *45* when the other cards are 89T even with two suited
>
> < *89* when the other cards are {543 or 542} all unsuited, or 432 even with two suited
>
> < *9T* when the other cards are 6 or lower, except {652 or 632} with two suited

The reason why SF2 [*56*, *67*, *78*] are never preferable to five new cards was discussed in the main text. It is not possible for these to be accompanied by three separately ranked other cards where at most one of them is a straight penalty at the extreme without one of them being a high card or two of them being a low pair.

Other Fine Video Poker Products from Bob Dancer

Million Dollar Video Poker *By Bob Dancer*

Bob Dancer is the best known video poker player and writer in the world. In just six years, after arriving in Las Vegas with a total bankroll of $6,000, Bob and his wife Shirley won more than $1 million in a six-month period playing video poker. His book, which recounts the events of those six years with stories about his meteoric ups and downs, has many lessons for players of all skill levels. Video poker is one of those rare casino games that can be beaten by a talented and informed player, and Bob explains how he did it. Never before has a top video poker professional shared so many of his winning secrets.

$16.95

Video Poker Winners Guides *By Bob Dancer and Liam W. Daily*

All Winners Guides cover both strategy and non-strategy aspects of play that are important for winner. Readers learn through the presentation and explanation of basic principles that take them through four levels of strategy.
Volume 1 – Jacks or Better (including 9/6, 9/5, 8/5, 8/5 with quads = 35, and 8/5 Bonus)
Volume 2 – Double Bonus (including 10/7, 9/7, and 10/7 with straight flush = 80)
Volume 3 – Full Pay Deuces Wild (also including "*pseudo* Full Pay Deuces Wild")
Volume 4 – NSU Deuces Wild (including 16/10/4/4/3 "Not So Ugly" and 15/9/4/4/3 "Ugly Ducks")
Volume 5 – Pick'em Poker

Volume 3-5 scheduled for release in early 2003. Volume 1 – 4: $16.50 each, Volume 5: $10

Bob Dancer Presents WinPoker Software *Created by Zamzow Software Solutions*

This software comes with 25 of the most popular video poker games in the casinos, including 9/6 Jacks or Better, 8/5 Bonus Poker, 10/7 Double Bonus, Jokers Wild, Deuces Wild, Double Double Bonus, Atlantic City Joker Poker, Pick 'em Poker and more. No other software compare for graphic quality, pre-loaded games, accuracy, and ease of use. There are also several variations of the new multiple-hand games, such as Triple Play.

Version 6.0 $29.95　　　　*Version 7.0 (scheduled release date 2003) $39.95*

Video Poker Strategy Cards
By Bob Dancer and Liam W. Daily

Excellent companions to the Dancer/Daily Winner's Guides, these video poker strategy cards may be the best strategy cards ever devised for any game. Four strategy levels take you from beginner to advanced, all on one six-panel tri-fold pocket-sized card. The "Beginner" strategies alone will improve almost anyone's play, while those who graduate to the "Advanced" strategies will be playing virtually as accurately as a computer. Carry the cards with you into the casinos and refer to them while you play. 9/6 Jacks or Better, 10/7 & 9/7 Double Bonus, Deuces Wild, Joker Wild, 8/5 Jacks & 8/5 Bonus, and 16/10 NSU Deuces Wild

$6.95 each or $35 for all six

You can purchase all these products at 10% off at
www.bobdancer.com